Mindfulness Therapy

Learn to Live a Happy and Fulfilling Life! Enjoy Every Moment

(De-stress and Find Transformative Peace and Happiness for Your Everyday Life)

Robert Everett

Published by Rob Miles

© **Robert Everett**

All Rights Reserved

Mindfulness Therapy: Learn to Live a Happy and Fulfilling Life! Enjoy Every Moment (De-stress and Find Transformative Peace and Happiness for Your Everyday Life)

ISBN 978-1-990084-04-1

All rights reserved. No part of this guide may be reproduced in any form without permission in writing from the publisher except in the case of brief quotations embodied in critical articles or reviews.

Legal & Disclaimer

The information contained in this book is not designed to replace or take the place of any form of medicine or professional medical advice. The information in this book has been provided for educational and entertainment purposes only.

The information contained in this book has been compiled from sources deemed reliable, and it is accurate to the best of the Author's knowledge; however, the Author cannot guarantee its accuracy and validity and cannot be held liable for any errors or omissions. Changes are periodically made to this book. You must consult your doctor or get professional medical advice before using any of the suggested remedies, techniques, or information in this book.

Upon using the information contained in this book, you agree to hold harmless the Author from and against any damages, costs, and expenses, including any legal fees potentially resulting from the application of any of the information provided by this guide. This disclaimer applies to any damages or injury caused by the use and application, whether directly or indirectly, of any advice or information presented, whether for breach of contract, tort, negligence, personal injury, criminal intent, or under any other cause of action.

You agree to accept all risks of using the information presented inside this book. You need to consult a professional medical practitioner in order to ensure you are both able and healthy enough to participate in this program.

Table of Contents

INTRODUCTION 7

CHAPTER 1: WHAT IS MINDFULNESS? 9

CHAPTER 2: FIRST STEPS TO MINDFULNESS 13

CHAPTER 3: THE FOUNDATIONS FOR MINDFULNESS 19

CHAPTER 4: SELF-CONFIDENCE THROUGH MINDFUL MEDITATION 28

CHAPTER 5: EVERYDAY MINDFULNESS 38

CHAPTER 6: EXERCISES 42

CHAPTER 7: MINDFULNESS MEDITATION AND BUDDHISM 50

CHAPTER 8: BENEFITS OF MINDFULNESS:BLESSINGS BEYOND THE SPIRITUAL 61

CHAPTER 9: HOW TO PRACTICE MINDFULNESS 67

CHAPTER 10: GETTING STARTED 71

CHAPTER 11: PEACE AND TRANQUILITY 78

CHAPTER 12: THE USE OF MINDFULNESS 81

CHAPTER 13: BEGINNING YOUR MINDFULNESS ADVENTURE 93

CHAPTER 14: UNIQUENESS OF LIVING IN THE PRESENT. 100

CHAPTER 15: THE MINDFULNESS SHORTCUT–TRAVEL ... 104

CHAPTER 16: MINDFULNESS FOR ALL 110

- CHAPTER 17: WHY BEING MINDFUL IS BENEFICIAL 119
- CHAPTER 18: PRACTICING MINDFULNESS MEDITATION 124
- CHAPTER 19: USING MINDFULNESS TO BECOME HAPPIER, PEACEFUL, AND FOCUSED 128
- CHAPTER 20: MINDFULNESS MEDITATION BENEFITS 137
- CHAPTER 21: PRACTICE MINDFUL OBSERVATION AND LISTENING 145
- CHAPTER 22: IN YOUR MIND'S EYE 151
- CHAPTER 23: DEALING WITH DISTRACTIONS WHILE MEDITATING 153
- CHAPTER 24: PRACTICING MINDFULNESS 158
- CHAPTER 25: HOW TO MAKE MEDITATION A HABIT 176
- CHAPTER 26: UNDERSTANDING ANXIETY 187
- CHAPTER 27: MINDFULNESS IN THE WORKPLACE 196
- CHAPTER 28: THE DARKER SIDE OF BEING MINDFUL – AND WHAT TO DO ABOUT IT 202
- CONCLUSION 209

Introduction

Known as a way to help you cope against negative thoughts and feelings, Mindfulness can also help you get to know yourself better, and allow you to have mastery of your thoughts and feelings—so you can finally live a stress-free life!

Mindfulness Meditation is amazing because it allows a non-judgmental observation of what's going on around you—so you can tap into the deepest parts of your soul. It allows you to live in the present moment, and turn off the negative thoughts in your head.

In this day and age, it's easy to fall into the traps of depression—which is why you have to find ways to let go of what plagues you, and meditation is something you can try to chase those blues away!

With the help of this book, you'll learn 25 meditation techniques that can take your stress away and help you live in the moment!

Read this book now and find out what they are!

Thanks again for downloading this book, I hope you enjoy it!

Chapter 1: What is Mindfulness?

Every day of your life offers opportunities. Some people are able to grasp these opportunities with both hands, are happy and seemingly fulfilled in their lives. These are the people who can walk past a garden of flowers and stop to take in the moment. Why? This is because they are very aware of their surroundings. If you were to observe people walking down a country lane, some would be mindful of their surroundings, while others may amble through the countryside and be so filled with other thoughts that the countryside is something they do not notice. Mindful people are always aware of their surroundings and appreciate them for the richness added to their lives.

Zen meditation, or Qi Gong are types of meditation that make the practitioner aware of their surroundings. In fact, focus is placed upon a certain object for a very good reason. This offshoot of meditation helps to focus that part of the brain which takes in information. At the front of the brain and at the cortex the activity within the brain helps awareness. This is the part of the brain that notices things and by practising mindful meditation and particularly the exercises of Zen meditation, you are training your mind to be observant and to be at one with its surroundings.

Mindful meditation is not something that can be forced. It needs to be practised but not to such an extent that the practitioner feels any obligation. In fact, once your mind is accustomed to this type of meditation, it becomes a natural instinct. When you took a sip of your coffee, were you thinking of something else? The chances are that you were getting through a busy day, sipped the coffee and carried on. Mindfulness is achieved by being totally aware of every action taken. Thus, the coffee example would go something like this.

- I am aware that I am holding a warm cup in my hand

- I am aware of the sense of aroma of fresh coffee
- I am aware of the tastes that hit the tongue and savor them
- I am aware that the cup is getting cooler
- I am aware that the coffee cup is empty

What people do when they are mindful is grasp every moment of their lives and become aware of that moment. This is what mindfulness is all about. All actions lead back to the mind, corcentrate on the breathing and you are totally aware of everything that you do and are centered so that you are in total control of yourself. This awareness is something which is lacking in today's world. People are too busy to be mindful.

One may question whether this is selfish or self centered. There are several ways to describe how this improves your life and selfishness is not one of them. If you are aware of yourself, your surroundings and are anchored in the moment, rather than going back over past experiences or anticipating too much, you are able to make that moment the best moment in your life. This enables you to give everyone around you the best of who you are. Thus, you will see the mindfulness is far from selfish. The selfish person is the person who drags others into their past or who pushes others to get what they want. That's a whole different ball game.

Once you learn mindfulness, you begin to see life from a different perspective. There are others who argue that the whole point of meditation is to empty the mind, though mindfulness is not contrary to meditation practice. It helps to hone the mind so that it can be totally at peace with the current moment and that's vital to any system of meditation. Without being grounded in that moment, how can the mind relax sufficiently to meditate?

This mindfulness prepares the mind to take on a new perspective which also allows total immersion in life, rather than extraction from it or seclusion away from it. Thus, these methods can be incorporated into modern day life to very great advantage.

Chapter 2: First Steps to Mindfulness

Mindfulness is a way of learning how to pay attention in a different way. It helps by bringing more focused attention on the tasks you would do normally, but with more focused attention. The emphasis is on observing what's happening, and allowing it, rather than trying to make anything different to how it already is.

As an introduction to ways that mindfulness can be practiced, try the following two exercises.

Eating the Grape

It might come as a surprise to realize that most of us don't pay much attention to what we eat. We may believe that, because we can feel the basic sensations of hunger, of chewing our food and the sensation of fullness in the stomach, we are aware. However, many people find, after trying out this exercise that there can much more involved in the simple act of eating.

Try this short exercise. You will be experimenting with mindful eating, and so follow the steps at a slower pace than you would normally take when eating something. At times, you might find your attention wandering. That's normal.If you feel your thoughts drifting off, bring your attention back to the grape. There is no wrong way to do this and it isn't wrong if you find yourself thinking of something else. It takes time and practice to learn to bring our attention to the present moment, even for short periods of time.

1. Take a grape (or raisin). Sit with your feet on the floor or in a position that's comfortable for you.

Breathe in and out three times, slightly slower than you normally would. This calms the body and helps to ground you in the moment.

2. Take hold of the grape, and try to really notice it. Notice how it feels in your hand. Notice if it's warm or cool. Is its surface soft or hard? Is it slippery? Try to imagine this is the first time you've ever seen a

grape. Try to notice it with a sense of curiosity.

3. Once you've looked at the grape for a short while, begin to roll it between your fingers. Notice how your fingers feel. How does the sensation of the grape's texture feel between them? After a few moments, you can close your eyes so that the physical sensations you feel will be clearer.

4. Once you have spent some time looking at the grape slowly bring your hand up to your mouth and place the grape onto your tongue. Hold the grape onto your tongue and examine how it feels. Try to feel the sensation of the flesh of the grape on your tongue. How does your breath feel? Can you feel it coming in and out of your nose?

5. Next begin to slowly chew the grape. Feel how it squishes between your teeth. Chew slowly and feel the juice running into other parts of your mouth. Can you feel it on your tongue? The insides of your cheeks? The roof of your mouth? What can you smell?

6. Keep chewing the grape past the point where you would normally swallow. Keep chewing slowly as you feel it disintegrate between your teeth.

7. When you feel a strong urge to swallow, then do. See what you can feel as you swallow. Can you feel your throat working? Your tongue? What sensations are passing through your mouth and body? What do you smell?

As you can see this is a very different way of eating! If you follow these instructions and practice experiencing such a simple act in this way, you can realize how different our experience is when we pay full attention to what is happening in our bodies.

Partial Body scan.

1. Sit in a chair with your feet on the floor, or in a position that's comfortable for you. For this partial scan we will use the hands, but if you would prefer to use a different part of your body, you may do so.

2. Rest your hands gently in your lap or by your sides. Breathe in and out for a few

moments. Again, remember that if you get distracted that's OK. Just bring your thoughts back to what you're doing as soon as you remember. Don't beat yourself up, you're not doing it wrong – everyone's mind wanders!

3. Start to become aware of your left hand. As you breathe in and out focus your attention on the back of the hand. Try to feel any sensation that is passing. Is it hot, or cold? Do you feel tingling or any kind of tension? If you don't feel anything, that's okay. Make a note of it.

4. Now extend your attention to your little finger on your left hand. Can you feel the place where it joins the hand? Can you feel your ring finger resting next to it, or the space between them if there is one? Do you have any other sensations? Try to feel the top, the back, the tip and the knuckle bones.

5. When you are ready, move your attention to the next finger along. Feel the passage of air over the skin. Feel for any warmth or coolness. Do you notice any

tingling or itching? Work to pay attention to what is happening in only that finger. When you are ready, move along to the next two fingers and thumb.

6. Focus now on the palm of your hand. Feel how it presses into the surface it is resting on. Is it tense? Is it warm? Cool? Do you feel anything at all?

7. Now try to feel your entire left hand. Notice your hand, from the nails of your fingers, to the creases in your palm and the bones and tendons inside your skin. Note any sensations, as well as any absence of sensation. There's no need to judge it. All you need to do is notice what you feel.

8. When you are ready, either finish the exercise, or move onto the right hand.

You may be surprised by how much detail and vividness you can perceive simply by noticing one part of your body.

Chapter 3: The Foundations for Mindfulness

Becoming mindful may seem simple and easy, but it is complex and takes time and dedication. To truly hone and develop your mindfulness practice, you must lay down a strong foundation for your practice. It will not always be so easy, and in fact, it can slip your mind quite often if you don't watch out, which is why a strong basic foundation is so important.

This chapter is about building a foundation for your mindfulness practice. Here, you will discover what it takes to support a true and lasting mindfulness practice with vital motivators and fortified commitment.

The Importance of Motivation and Intention

To be truly on your way to mindfulness, you need to forge a sound daily practice of mindfulness meditation. Simple as it is though, it isn't always easy, which is why motivation is so important. You need to explore your intentions and the goals that keep you motivated in continuing your practice. By having clear intentions and motivations, you can develop a strong and unwavering commitment to your practice.

Delving into intentions

Intention means purpose, or whatever you hope to achieve through your efforts. No matter what you have been led to believe, intention always has an effect on how you do something.

For example, if you are volunteering at a local soup kitchen because you just want extra credits for an assignment, you go about your work differently than if you volunteer because you truly want to help people. The reasons behind why you are endeavoring can make your endeavors purposeful or meaningless, and the quality of your work changes as well.

Another example is driving to work. If your intention at driving is to get to work safely, then it would follow that you would drive carefully. However, if your intention is to get there as soon as possible, then you can end up driving recklessly and putting yourself and others in danger.

The truth is that intention, or purpose, changes the nature of what you are doing, even if the act itself is still the same. Your intentions strongly affect everything you do, more so your meditation practices.

The Importance of Intentions

When it comes to mindfulness, there are three key components that go hand in hand. These are attention - keeping your focus, attitude - doing it with a particular set of ideals, and intention - your purpose. Intention is often the most disregarded but it is extremely important.

Intention can make your practice much more fulfilling and encompassing, as intention evolves along with your consciousness. Many people start out with rather simplified intention, such as getting better sleep or reducing anxiety. It is perfectly alright for you to start with a simple purpose such as these, and indeed many people do start mindfulness with these intentions. However, as their consciousness and awareness evolve, their intentions can also become deeper and more meaningful.

Do not forget that in original Buddhist teachings, mindfulness was developed as a way to feel, and have empathy and compassion for all. As you develop your practice, the ultimate intention that you can hold is to have love to spare for all things, and the desire to end all suffering.

Techniques for Finding your Intention

Writing your future self

A good way to find out what you really want to achieve is to write to your future self. This exercise will allow you to become honest with yourself when it comes to the things you want to achieve and improve.

Reflect on what you want to achieve in five to ten years. Write about the attitudes and behavior that you would like to improve. Allow yourself to dream and write about it. Ask a friend to mail the letter to you at a random date in the next year.

Finishing Sentences

This exercise gives you time to look into yourself and your intentions with a bit more formality. Take a piece of paper and write down these questions:

With mindfulness meditation I hope to...

Through mindfulness I can...

I hope that practicing mindfulness will make me...

The best I aim to achieve in mindfulness is...

Next, focus on one question and give yourself a minute or two to write down as many answers to these questions as you can. From there, look at your answers. Try to weigh them and see if any of the answers surprise you. Take another piece of paper and write down the ones you feel are most compelling. This will give you something to go back on when you feel like your motivation is wavering.

Building Up-strong Commitment

When you make a commitment to something, you are making a promise to that person or endeavor, and to yourself. Commitment is about following through with your promises and persisting despite hardship. If you truly want to achieve something, you need to have some amount of commitment to the cause and to your own dreams and goals. Without commitment, the first real problems or bumps in the road can dissuade you from continuing to pursue your goal. Without commitment, your dreams will remain dreams only.

It is the same with mindfulness. For you to really make a difference in your life with mindfulness, you have to be committed. This means you have to believe in mindfulness and what it can help you achieve. You cannot make a commitment without belief and trust.

Making the commitment is the easy part; it is following through and the actual doing that is the most difficult of all. It can be difficult to sit quietly for 10 to 15 minutes when you've been feeling stressed and pressured at work. During times like this, a lot of people just want a cold beer or some wine while watching TV.

What keeps you going into your corner and doing your meditations? Your commitment and belief that in the long run, meditation will help you better deal with stress than cod beers ever can.

Simple tips to stay determined in your practice

Don't be too hard on yourself - Sometimes, when you're really serious about something, it can be hard to forgive yourself for a slip up early on. You may end up losing faith in yourself and losing interest in mindfulness altogether. Remember that meditation and mindfulness both take time and are long-term processes that have to be fine-tuned to suit you. Be patient and keep going, even if you do skip a day or two sometimes.

Trust in yourself - One of the best ways to keep your determination up is when you have someone who believes in your eventual success, and who can better do that than you! You have to have faith in your abilities and your own success.

Take it one step at a time -Try not to overwhelm yourself in everything you expect to change in your lie. As mentioned before, mindfulness is simply about the experience and not the outcome. Remember to take things step by step. You can't expect to make a major life change after a few sessions. Take simple steps and cherish the experience.

Make realistic commitments

One of the reasons it can be hardto make a commitment is because you're not ready for it, or you've gotten too ambitious. Although it may be a good idea to aim high, aiming too high can set you up for failure and disappointment. Such feelings can make you resent the idea of meditation, and you may end up anticipating it with a lot of negativity. This is why setting up realistic commitments is so important.

Take things easy in the beginning, and as you get better at it, you can start to challenge yourself more and more. Make sure that your daily meditation fits in with your life harmoniously while also serving your needs. If you find that your life is too hectic and you have a busy schedule, then making a commitment to two hours of meditation a day probably won't fit the bill. Try doing 10-minute meditations twice a day, once upon waking and once before bed. You can even add a 15-minute eating meditation in there when you feel ready.

As you continue practicing meditation regularly, no matter how brief, it will become a habit, instead of a chore. It will become easier to do and will be a welcome rest in your day. Soon, you will be feeling odd when you miss a session because meditation has become such a regular part of your routine. Of course, just because you've reached this point doesn't mean there won't be times you won't feel like going through with it. However, you can just keep going anyway, more from enjoyment and fulfillment, which also strengthens your commitment.

Chapter 4: SELF-CONFIDENCE THROUGH MINDFUL MEDITATION

One of the noticeable outcomes of Mindfulness is self-confidence. Mindfulness is a morale booster. Every attempt of being mindful of yourself and your surroundings, it will have a positive effect on your well-being. As we make Mindfulness a way of life, we are transforming into a better person and able to influence others around us in a good way.

It is quite interesting to understand that self-confidence can be developed through Mindfulness or mindful meditation. Some scientific statistics show that any activities that centric on mindful meditation may turn out boosting the self-esteem of the subject.

Some organizations recognise positive effects of Mindfulness on individual and willing to invest in Mindfulness program for the well-being of their employees. Before diving into the main subject of how

Mindfulness can instil self-confidence, it is important to define what self-confidence really is. Someone once said that a self-confident person is someone who can manage his ego; such a person can be humble when there is need to learn something important and he does not consider himself most important or least significance. The subject knows his boundaries, respect others and learn from others with meekness. This is something most people are yet to understand. True self-confidence is not looking down on oneself, do not considering oneself too important in any situations and do not take failure as failure but a part of learning process (i.e. failure is failure until you give up) and has ability to keep learning until success can be mastered. Hence, we can define self-confidence:

Self-confidence is the ability to believe in oneself to do anything and do not limited by resources at the present moment.

Now, we are in a better position to answer the question we asked earlier: how can you build self-confidence through mindfulness meditation? The answer is THROUGH MINDFUL AWARENESS and MINDFUL COMPASSION.

Self-awareness and self-compassion are foundations of building self-confidence. It is only when you can understand your strengths, your weaknesses and learn not to judge yourself, then you will be able to have self-confidence for your daily life and start to live.

GETTING READY FOR THE NEXT 7 DAYS

So much has already been said on Mindfulness. If you are an enthusiastic reader, I will not be surprised that you are all ready to start the next 7 days' practice; after all the most important thing is the practice itself. Wait, just relax and read on.

Prior to the 7 days' practice, there are some principles to take note and help you to overcome challenges of starting a new skill, for practicing mindfulness will need some disciplines and commitments, so how to start mindfulness meditation?

Here are five things which you may want to keep in mind while practising Mindfulness meditation:

Focus

The challenge of mindful meditation is to focus on your breathing. If your mind is not able to free from a thought, it is well. You do not need to be too concern, for your mind knows how to adjust itself when you concentrate on your breathing alone. Though a thought may come and go, acknowledge your feeling, do not judge it, and just keep your mind on your breathing. Mindfulness meditations are non-judgemental of self and have self-compassion. Focus on each breath.

Persevere

Never give up. Practice create a habit; good habit come with persistent practices and lots of patience. Even if you missed a practice once a while, just keep going and practise mindful meditation every day. Then one day, you will realise that it has become part of your daily living and will notice those benefits which brings to your life.

Get a partner

Although you can be a lone ranger, it is always more fun when you practise Mindfulness with a friend or a colleague. Hook up with anyone that has a similar interest and agree to a time that is convenient for both of you to enjoy the Mindfulness meditation and sharing experience together.

Have a goal

Whenever embarking on any Mindfulness meditation or practice, try not to focus on how well you practice. Instead your mind should be on what you are going to learn and discover through the practice.

Appreciate yourself

Appreciate yourself for every successful practice you accomplished. It is not easy to arrange time out of your busy schedule for something like this. Nevertheless, it brings great benefit for you if you do. You just need a few minutes every day for each exercise. Thank yourself at the end of each exercise and say to yourself, "Thank you. You have done well".

TAKING CARE OF YOUR BREATHING

Slow down your breathing and observe your breathing is a good way to stabilise your disturbed feelings and calm your chattering mind. You will need approximately 11 minutes every day for at least 1 week. The simple 7 days' challenge will transform your life. Prolong practise mindfulness enhances your physical health, improve your mental strength and self-confidence.

The feeling of anxiety, anger and stress will affect your well-being; if you constantly dwelling in them, it will not only impair your health, they will also reduce our abilities to make sound decisions from time to time. This is why practicing mindfulness becomes important for us to stay calm and relax at most of the time in our lives especially when we feel the pressure at work rising around and within us. Mindfulness is one of the most effective ways to combat troubling feelings through awareness, curb it and transform it in your mental system. Paying close attention to what goes on inside of you can improve your health, make you more resilient to stress and help you to gain more control of your life.

The upcoming exercises will empower your mind to manage your thoughts in a better manner. The ultimate effect will often be a clearer mind and a happier heart.

The first practice you will be doing for the first day is learning to focus on your breathing. It is to help you cultivate Mindfulness meditation through your breathing. By taking care of your breathing, which also known as mindful breathing, it helps you to deal with all troublesome feelings and emotions inside you. In the end of a mindful breathing session, you will experience inner peace and stillness, your ability to concentrate will improve and you will be able to work a little more comfortably under extreme conditions. Thus, you will be able to exist apart from those feelings and thoughts that would have weighed you down, thereby having more tolerance for any difficulties.

Taking care of your breathing will help you stay focused even amidst so many distractions. One may ask how paying attention to breathing can reduce stress and help one remain present in the moment? It may not make so much sense but taking care of your breathing really works; practise no judgement for that thought. You will experience freedom from worries of life which can be overwhelming. This freedom can become a way of living everyday if you can practise mindfulness consistently.

Mindfulness practice through breathing is basically accomplished by paying attention to how you inhale and exhale. Whichever position you choose to take during practice is up to you, choose a position that is comfortable to you; however, you may find a comfortable position can be either lying down or sitting down position, and remember to straight up your back.

After you have chosen a position, you are ready to do the 1st day's practice.

1st Day's Practice

Start by closing your eyes.

Take a deep breath.

Breathe-in for 4 seconds, count 4-3-2-1 then hold your breath for 2 seconds, count 2-1 and then breathe-out for 6 seconds, count 6-5-4-3-2-1.

Do this repeatedly for 12 times

Take your time and feel the air in and out of your nostril.

Notice and observe any sensation on your body.

Acknowledge it by saying: "This is (the feeling you are feeling now)."

If your mind wanders away, do not try to judge it.

Gradually shift your focus back to your breathing.

You have learnt the breathing technique and may use it for relaxation purpose. Any time you feel anxious, you may practise the breathing technique.

Chapter 5: Everyday Mindfulness

Doing Laundry

This is something we have to do, but you can make the chore of folding it a mindful exercise.

Take time to feel the materials before you fold them. How do they feel on your skin? Take extra care when you fold them, paying attention to how the material reacts when you're folding it and what your reaction is when it does not fold quite right. Stop when you feel yourself getting frustrated and ask yourself why it is unnerving. Then, visualize another way to fold it. Do this with each piece, taking the time note how you feel as the pile of laundry is diminishing.

While putting it away, take special interest in how it slips onto the hanger or the sound the drawer makes when you open and close it. Think about how you place the articles of clothing in the drawers as you are putting them away. Don't let anything else distract you.

Cooking

Smell each herb before you add it to the dish. Note how they make you react to the aroma as it travels up your nose and through your olfactory senses. Imagine what the dish will taste like once it is added. Do this with each seasoning. Feel the knife as you cut the ingredients you prepare for the dish.

How does the knife feel in your hand? How does it feel as it cuts through the meat or vegetable?

Hear the water boil. What does it remind you of? The ocean? A bubbling stream?

Listen to the ingredients when they hit the pan you are using to sear them. Take notice of how you feel in the moment when you hear the sizzle.

As you stir a pot, close your eyes and concentrate on the motion of the spoon stirring the contents. Does it relax you?

Eating

Instead of gulping it down, take the time to move the food around in your mouth.How does it taste?What is the texture?How does the overall experience of eating make you feel?

See if you can taste the individual flavors.What do you like about how the tastes mingle?It is not necessary to do it throughout the meal, just the first bites.

Listening to Music

We all have music in our lives playing the background as we go about our day.It's the sound in distance as we vacuum or dust.

Stop what you are doing.Close your eyes.Let your senses hear, feel, and live the music.Pay attention to how each note, each measure and verse affects you.If you feel you need to sit down, do so.If you feel you need to sway, do so.Drown out all other noises and just listen to the music and how it makes you feel.Live in the music.Do this for a few songs.

Change the station or playlist to something else you like to listen to.How does this change in music make you feel?

Taking a shower

Step under the water; close your eyes, and let it wash over you, down through your hair, neck shoulders, back and to your toes.How does the water feel as it makes its way to the drain?How does it feel as it rolls down from your crown to your feet?

Envision the water flowing through you, not around you.Imagine it taking all the aches and stresses of the day down the drain as it makes its journey.Do you feel more relaxed?

If you are taking a cool shower, how does it feel as it changes temperature while making its way to the drain?Does it feel refreshing?Do you feel invigorated?

Getting Dressed

We all do this in a rush, but when you slow down and take it in, how do you feel?What is the sensation that you experience as the material slides across your skin to its resting place?What are you feeling when it finally settles onto your skin?When you're walking, does it feel any different?

Chapter 6: Exercises

When our mind feels as if it's constantly being pulled from every corner, our thoughts become scattered and chaotic which in turn, affects the way we feel. This could leave us feeling overwhelmed and completely exhausted. In some cases, it can also make us feel irritable and easily angered, causing our tempers to flare up unnecessarily which, if left unchecked, can even damage our relationships.

Typically, the solution for this is to take some time off and get away from everything. However, not everyone can afford this luxury. For a lot of us, working continuously is a basic demand and taking care of our well-being becomes the least of our priorities. Now, you don't need a lengthy vacation to keep your mental health in check. All you really need is about 10 to 30 minutes of free time to indulge in a healing meditation that will put you back in a relaxed and mindful state.

It doesn't take a lot and this particular amount of time will not eat too much into your daily schedule. Remember, it is essential to put ourselves first, lest we end up burning out and being unable to do anything at all. Take care of your mind and body by doing these simple exercises everyday.

Mindful Breathing

When it comes to doing this exercise, note that you have the option to do it whilst standing up or sitting down. You can do it just about anywhere at any given time, as long as you're able to focus your mind and be still. Your concentration should all be on your breath for at least one whole minute.

Start breathing in and out slowly. A cycle of this should last for about 6 seconds. Breathe in through your nose and exhale through your mouth, allowing the air to flow freely into your body. Let go of any thoughts that you have, any pending projects or task that you still need to do. Be still.

This is the simplest form of meditation.

Mindful Observation

Simple yet very powerful, this exercise truly allows you to be in the moment and is designed to help you reconnect with the environment that you are in. Best done in the outdoors, this will enable you to better appreciate the beauty of the small things you often miss due to your everyday rush. It could be anything from the beautiful view of the city that you pass during commutes or something simpler, such as a garden that you see everyday but rarely pause for. It can also be applied during more relaxed moments; whilst you're on vacation and wanting to savor every moment of it.

To begin, simply pick a natural object within your surroundings. Focus on it and simply watch it for a minute or two. Allow yourself to fall into a relaxing state of mind, explore the image and take in even the smallest detail. As you do this, imagine your energy merging with this object.

Connect with it and its simplicity of simply being.

Mindful Awareness

This particular exercise is meant to help us develop better appreciation and awareness when it comes to our daily tasks as well as its results.

To begin, think of something that's an everyday occurrence. A small thing that you often take for granted such as opening the windows at morning, watering the plants and even the mere act of sweeping. The next time you do any of these things, pay attention to what you're doing - to the way the air feels on your face when you open the window, the smell of the plants after you water them and the sound of the broom while you sweep. Focus on these things and allow it to take you away while you do the task. It's simple, but you'll definitely feel better about doing these things after.

Mindful Listening

Aside from using your sense of sight to develop mindfulness, you can also make use of your sense of hearing to further immerse yourself in this state of mind. This exercise is designed to enable you to open your ears to different sounds and listen in a non-judgmental way. Did you know that a lot of what we hear on a daily basis are influenced by past experiences? To prevent fear, worry and anxiety due to this, we must learn how to listen while being neutral about it. To be aware, but to hear things without any preconceived notions.

To begin, choose music that you have never listened to before. Put on your headphones and listen to it. Don't think about anything else about it other than the sound you're hearing. If you happen to dislike it, let go of this feeling and allow the music to take over your thoughts.

Mindful Immersion

For this, the goal is to cultivate our contentment of the quiet moments and not chase after the adrenaline we get from always being busy. It's about being still and not looking for anything to do, simply enjoying the silence and allowing our mind to relax from the everyday chaos that it goes through. In doing this, we can avoid the anxiousness associated with wanting to finish tasks or catching up with deadlines. It provides clarity and restores our focus so that we can do more in the present.

Example, while you're making food for yourself or your family, try and focus on every detail of the task. Instead of rushing through it mindlessly, think about your ingredients and the process of preparation. By doing this, not only are you being present; you will also find better and more efficient ways of doing things. It's as if you're rediscovering the activity and experiencing it for the first time again.

This takes out the tediousness of doing something fairly routine and makes everything a lot more enjoyable.

Mindful Appreciation

For this, what you need to do is take note of 5 different things that happen in your daily life. These need to be things that typically go unappreciated or something that you don't really give much thought to. The goal here is to instil a sense of appreciation and gratitude for the small things in your life. These are the people or things that provide you with comfort and support whenever you need it, but also get neglected as you search for bigger things.

For example: take note of the person who delivers your mail or your daily paper, think of the clothes that give you warmth or the birds that sing to you each morning. Now ask yourself these questions:

Are you aware of how these things came to be and how they work?

Have you ever acknowledged how these small things benefit your life as well as that of others?

Can you imagine life without these things?

Have you paid attention to how complex these things are and that they have finer details that you once missed?

Have you ever spent time thinking about how these things connect with you and the environment? Ever thought of the role they play when it comes to the bigger picture?

Why do this? It may not seem like much at first, but repetition will help you develop a better appreciation and understanding of the environment around you. This also includes better self-awareness as you're able to tune out what's not needed and focus more on the things that matter. It's all about really seeing the world around you without any judgment or bias, to simply appreciate things as they were created.

Chapter 7: Mindfulness Meditation and Buddhism

Anyone can practice mindfulness even without Buddhism; however, Buddhists cannot practice their doctrine without mindfulness. This is because in Buddhism, "mindfulness" is synonymous with meditation. More often than not, mindfulness denotes the practice of intentional awareness of an individual's thoughts and actions without judgment in the present moment. It is employed both to the thoughts and feelings of the mind and the actions of the body.

In Buddhism, mindfulness is deemed as requirement for one's development of wisdom and insight. In the Noble Eightfold Path, right mindfulness is the seventh path while in the Four Noble Truths, it is the fourth truth.

Right mindfulness is also called the Right Meditation. There are a number of forms of both mindfulness and meditation. For instance, mentally providing a verbal name or label to every in breath and out breath on a sitting meditation is an example of mindfulness.On the other hand, an individual does not necessarily need to conduct a formal meditation session in order to apply mindfulness. Mindfulness is applied through allowing the mind to focus on what transpires in the present moment and at the same time being aware of the usual "commentary" of the mind.

Furthermore, mindfulness is done any time without being required to sit in a corner.For example, an individual can be mindful of the sounds of the wind; of the sensations in his feet as he walks; or the texture of soapy water as he does dishes.This denotes being mindful what happens in the present moment and at the same time, being aware of the commentary of the mind.

Meditation has benefits, alleviation for anxiety and stress being included in this. Consider what you want to accomplish with your meditation. People come to deep breathing for an array of reasons -

whether to boost their creativeness, help visualize an objective, quiet their internal chatter, or make a religious connection. In case your only goal is to invest a few momentsevery day being within the body without fretting about all you want to do, that's reason enough to meditate.

Look for a distraction-free area. Particularly when you're just getting started, it's important to clear your environment of distracting feelings. Change off it and radio, close your home windows against the road noises outside, and close your door to noisy roommates. In the event that you talk about your house with roommates or family, you may find it difficult to find a quiet space where you can concentrate on meditation. Ask individuals your home is with if indeed they would be willing to keep silent throughout your meditation exercise. Guarantee to come inform them when you're completed, to allow them to resume their normal activities.

A scented candle, a bouquet of flowers, or incense can be great little details to improve your deep breathing experience.

Come out the lamps to help you focus.

Use a meditation cushion. Deep breathing cushions are also called zafus. A zafu is a round cushion which allows you to take a seat on the bottom while meditating. Since it doesn't have a back again, like a seat will, it doesn't enable you to slump back again and lose concentrate on your energy. In the event that you don't have a zafu, any old cushion or sofa pillow can do to keep you from getting sore during long exercises of cross-legged seated.

If you discover that sitting without a chair-back hurts your back, feel absolve to use a seat. Try to be there within you and keep maintaining a right back for so long as it feels comfortable, then slim back again until you are feeling you are able to do it again.

Wear comfortable clothes. You don't want anything to draw you out of your meditative considering, so avoid restrictive clothing that may pull you, like jeans or limited pants. Consider what you may wear to exercise or even to rest in - those types of loose, breathable clothes are your very best bet.

Select a time when you're comfortable. When you're more acquainted with meditation, you might utilize it to calm you down when you're feeling anxious or overwhelmed. But if you're a newbie, you might find it hard to focus initially if you're not in the right mindset. When you're getting started, meditate when you already feel calm - perhaps very first thing each day, or after you've needed to unwind after college or work.

Remove every distraction you can think of before you sit back to meditate. Get a light treat if you're feeling starving; use the restroom if you want to, etc.

Have a timer accessible. You intend to make sure you practice your meditation for long enough, nevertheless, you also don't want to break your focus by checking enough time. Arranged a timer for the amount of time you intend to meditate - whether ten minutes or one hour. Your telephone may have an integral timer onto it, or you can find many websites and applications that will time your sessions for you.

Meditating

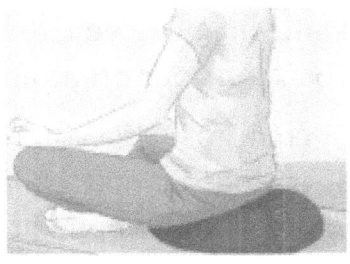

Take a seat on your cushioning or seat with a right back. The upright posture allows you to focus on your inhaling and exhaling as you purposefully breathe in and out. If you're seated in a seat with a back again, do not lean back again against it or slouch. Stay as erect as you possibly can.

Position your legs in whichever manner is comfortable for you. You can lengthen them out before you or mix them beneath you prefer a pretzel if you're utilizing a cushion on the floor. The main thing is that your position remains right. Don't fret in what regarding the hands. In the press, we often see people keeping their hands at their knees when meditating, but if that's uncomfortable for you, don't be concerned about it. You are able to fold them in your lap, let them suspend at your edges - whatever gives you to clear your brain and focus on your breathing.

Tilt your chin as if you're looking downward. It doesn't matter if your eye are opened up or shut when you meditate, though many people think it is easier to filter visual interruptions with closed eye. Either real way, tilting your mind as if you're looking down helps start the upper body and simplicity your breathing.

Arranged your timer. When you're in an appropriate position and will be ready to get started, arranged your timer for however long you'd prefer to meditate. Don't feel any pressure to attain an hour-long transcendental condition throughout your first week. Start small with 3-5 minute classes, and work the right path up to around 30 minutes, or even much longer if you'd like.

Keep the mouth area shut as you breathe. You should both breathe in and out through your nasal area when meditating. However, ensure that your jaw muscles are calm, even though the mouth area is shut. Don't clench your jaws or grind your tooth; simply relax. Concentrate on your inhaling and exhaling. This is exactly what meditation's about. Rather than attempting never to take into account the things that may stress you from a day-to-day basis, give yourself something positive to spotlight: your breathing.

Focus on your sucking in just how that's preferred for you. Some people like to concentrate on how the lungs expand and contract, while others prefer to think about how exactly air goes by through the nasal area when they breathe.

You might even concentrate on the sound of your breathing. Just bring you to ultimately circumstances of brain where you're exclusively centered on some facet of your breathing.

Notice your breath, but analyze it don't. The target is to be there within each breathing, not to have the ability to explain it. Don't worry about remembering what you're sense, or having the ability to explain the knowledge at another time. Just experience each breathing in as soon as. When it goes by, go through the next breathing. Do not take into account the deep breathing with your brain - just experience it through your senses.

Bring your attention back again to your breath if it wanders. Even though you've gained a great deal of experience with meditation, you'll find that your ideas might wander. You'll start considering work or expenses or the errands you have to perform later. Whenever you spot the outside world creeping in, don't stress and make an effort to disregard them. Instead, softly nudge your concentrate back to the feeling of your breathing within you, and let other thoughts again fall away.

You may find it simpler to maintain your concentrate on inhalations than on exhalations. Keep this at heart if you discover it to be true. Try to focus especially on the sensation of your breathing as it leaves the body.

Try counting your breaths if you're having difficulty refocusing your attention.

Don't be too much on yourself. Accept that concentrate will be hard for you when you're just getting started. Don't berate yourself- all beginners go through the internal chatter. Actually, some would say that continual go back to today's instant is the "practice" of deep breathing. Furthermore, don't expect your meditation practice to improve your daily life overnight. Mindfulness does take time to exert its impact. Keep returning to deep breathing every day for at least a few moments, lengthening your periods when possible.

Chapter 8: Benefits of Mindfulness:Blessings Beyond the Spiritual

Many people take up practicing mindfulness as a part of their unique spiritual path, and it is definitely a very good way to begin such a journey. Spiritual experts often express the sentiment that the surest way to enlightenment is to embrace and live every moment of your life in the here and now. While this seems true for many who have made that choice, there is also more to mindfulness than a way to develop spiritually.

Stress Reduction

The first benefit you're likely to notice is a significant reduction in your response to stressful situations. You're living in the here and now – the only time and place where you truly have any power to make and act on decisions. This frees you from any frustration you're giving in to when you dwell on the past or future. Psychiatric care programs often teach mindfulness to help patients reduce their stress. And even medical care treatment centers use mindfulness techniques to help their patients deal with the stress involved with being sick.

Emotional Stability

Another reason psychiatric treatment centers teach mindfulness is that it can greatly improve your emotional stability. By relieving stress and keeping you focused on today's events, you respond with more wisdom and flexibility. Although you'll still have feelings, some of them negative like anger or fear, they'll be in your conscious awareness where you can manage them and use them to make the most of every opportunity to choose your higher good.

Reality-Based Thinking

Many spiritual leaders and philosophers are fond of saying that there's really no objective reality. Reality, according to them, is entirely based on your own perspective. In an experiential way, this is entirely true. However, you do have your own version of reality. When you stray from that, you invite paranoid, obsessive and delusional thinking.

On the other hand, when you're wholly present in each moment, you see reality more clearly. Noticing the facts and sensations of the present moment helps you stay in touch with what's real. That's not to say that you can't have non-reality-based thoughts now. It just means that if you do, you're not living mindfully.

Weight Loss

Living mindfully can also help you lose weight. To accomplish this, you practice mindful eating. In a later chapter, you can learn how to approach your eating habits with a mindfulness awareness of whether you're really hungry or not. You can also find out how to eat mindfully to enjoy your food more and reduce or eliminate the amount of eating you do without being fully aware of the experience.

Physical Healing

Being mindful can promote healing and help you regain your health. How does it work? Because you're practicing mindfulness with the wisdom of discernment, you have the clarity of mind to make the best medical decisions to speed your healing. Beyond that, your immune system and nervous system work better when you're in touch with your anger, fear or confusion about the illness. This happens because you're not pushing down your feelings into your subconscious where they can damage your health.

Everything you experience has a bearing on the health of your body. And it isn't just having the experience that matters. Instead, it's finding acceptance of your body the way it is and the possible outcomes, both positive and negative. Otherwise, those feelings simmer on the back burner. They build up and grow over time. You're not consciously aware of them, so you can't deal with them in the here and now.

Recent research into how much mindfulness can promote healing has been extremely convincing. In fact, the practice of it has been taught to patients in hospitals and incorporated into inpatient treatments for diseases as serious as cancer and heart disease along with other diseases and conditions that are more directly related to stress.

Help with Chronic Medical Conditions

Chronic medical conditions can pose a significant threat to your health and shorten your life. They can also make day-to-day life miserable. Staying in touch with this present moment can help you shift your focus away from past worries about your condition and the pain it causes. As you release your stress, increase your emotional stability and lose excess weight, chronic conditions become more manageable.

Mindfulness to Increase Your Success

Whether you're a student or you've already started your climb on the corporate ladder, you can be more successful by practicing mindfulness. As you do, you are more keyed in on your boss's or teacher's instructions and expectations. You see more quickly what you need to do and can act in the now to effect change. Thus, you become a much better student or employee, which leads you to succeed in school, work and all aspects of your life.

Chapter 9: How to Practice Mindfulness

Building up a sense of calm and relaxation get into the position that you have chosen to practice your Mindfulness in.One you are settled into your position, then you check the four foundations of Mindfulness, which are referred to as the four frames of positions that you may study.You may try them one at a time, or in tandem, or even all at once.

1.Body-Mindfulness.During body-mindfulness you will explore your body, taking mental notes, exploring the various components that make up your body such as head, hair, muscles, teeth, skin, heart, bones, stomach, etc.During this practice you are to focus on what it is they are doing, where they are, and what they are dependant on etc.

Focus on all of the individual parts of your body and observe them.You may discover that a part of your body you are observing becomes clearer to you in another way.

Part of Mindfulness of the body is focusing on "breathing in and breathing out."

Studying the way certain body parts react to movement or other events, can help you to understand why you are feeling tired, or have muscle tension etc.

Without the mind the body is just meat and bones, it needs the mind to control its actions.

Study the physical characteristics of a body part—like what it is either a liquid or a solid for example.

2.Mindfulness of Sensations and Physical Feelings.Often this is referred to as body-states meditation.

Important to learn how to focus on how sensations in the human body occur.Take note mentally of where or when different feelings are occurring.You need to study how the body and mind are interacting during different feelings.

A technique that can be used in both (body-focused) meditations is to scan your body, watch how the energy flows, or pass the energy to new part of the body.

This is a skill that helps to reduce tension just by relaxing your body, and to mentally let go of the pressures and tensions that are arising, and to increase the level of tolerance your body has and the understanding of its nature.

3.Mindfulness of Mental States.This area covers fantasies, images, thoughts, dreams, ideas, etc.Try to focus on how they occurred, was it because of feelings you had, or was it due to outside influences?You can become aware of how thoughts and feelings can change from one way to another.

4.Mindfulness of the Consciousness.This area of Mindfulness might include such things as your state of mind as in being energetic, unfocused, tired, peaceful, or anxious etc.

To help to give you an awareness of your mind there are questions you can ask yourself being the following:"Is my mind desiring or rejecting something?" or "Is my mind being dominated by feelings of anger or greed?"

Chapter 10: Getting Started

Mindfulness meditation is different from other forms of meditation because it does not mean to change you. Instead, it develops your deep awareness for what you already have, moment by moment. It somehow brings you to a state of being "unconditionally present", so that you become focused on the "now".

Basic Mindfulness Meditation Guide

There are three basic aspects that need to be worked on in this meditation technique: your body, your breath, and then your thoughts.

Body

Let's discuss about relating with your body first. This will include setting up the area where you will be practicing daily. This is an important aspect because the area you will choose and the environment where you will practice will affect the difficulty of your practice.

Since you are going to use this meditation technique to prepare yourself for working with other people, this will be an eyes-open practice; making what is in front of you and around you as important considerations. You need not make an entire room for meditation; if you do not have a spare room at home you can just use a corner of your bedroom or any space in the house where you can experience some peace and quiet.

Some people build a small "altar" of photos or sacred objects based on their tradition or religion; you may also do so if you want. If you think that these objects won't beneficial, you may just light candles or incense just to set the mood. But if you simply want a plain wall, it's okay, as well. The idea is just to get you away from things that would distract you, like the television or your laptop. As long as you can achieve that sense of relaxation and concentration with minimal to no distraction, that area would have served its purpose.

Once you have identified an ideal spot, you will have to choose where you will sit. You may can use a cushion on the floor or you can sit on a chair. If you don't have a cushion, you can simply fold up one or two blankets or a low bench. The idea is for you to sit comfortably, without the distraction of wiggly chairs.

If you are sitting on a chair, be sure to get one that has a flat seat and has a straight back rest. If you are short and you will find it uncomfortable, place a foot rest on the floor so that you take a little bit of your weight out. It is not ideal to have your legs and feet dangling uncomfortably. On the other hand, if you are tall, ensure that your hips are positioned higher than your knees, you can use a chair or a cushion to achieve this position. This will prevent from straining your back easily.

Next on your list is to establish your posture. You will have to be on an upright posture but make sure it is not too rigid; keep your chin up, your chest out, and your back straight with a little curve in the lower back. Use a "dignified" posture, but not necessarily stiff. If this works for you, then you don't have to worry about an aching back after.

If you are using a cushion, you can cross your legs, only if you are comfortable. When you are doing this, make sure to add more height to the cushion or add more blankets.

Your hands should rest comfortably on your thighs, with your palms facing down. You need your eyes to be open. You will have to fix your gaze on the floor in front of you, about 4 to 6 feet away. If you are closer to a wall in that same distance, you can fix your sight on the wall wherever it lands, as if you were looking at a distance.

You don't need to keep your gaze tightly focused; the idea is to gaze into whatever is in front of you. Let your eyes rest on the floor, or wall, or object.

Start by sitting in your preferred position for a few minutes, trying out the environment. Focus your gaze and if you notice your attention beginning to wander, gently bring it back to your own body and the environment. Do not do things abruptly; the keyword is to do them as gently as possible. Expect your mind to wander, that is a part of who you are, you just have to keep on coming back each time your mind and attention wander away.

Breath

The next aspect that we have to work on is your breath or your breathing. For this practice, lightly rest your attention on your breath. Be aware as it air enters and as it goes out of your body. You don't need to learn a special breathing technique for this, but it just have to be as rhythmically and as normally as possible. The idea is not to force inhaling and exhaling. You don't have to manipulate your breathing. In case you notice that you are beginning to control your breathing, just let it be. Don't worry about it, just let go. Remember, "lightly" focus your attention on your breathing? You don't need to think about your breathing technique here.

So, again, for starters, sit for a few minutes, going into a comfortable position, being aware of the environment, and now "lightly" focusing on your breathing – inhale and exhale, inhale and exhale. Make sure you don't focus all your attention to your breathing because the rest of your attention should also be on your own body and your environment.

Thoughts

The last aspect is working on your own thoughts. While you are in position, you will notice that many thoughts will arise. Some would be great thoughts, and then some overlapping one another, there will be memories of the past and plans about the future, there may also be daydreams, or even the commercials you have seen on TV.

These thoughts will be a lot but you will have to go back and feel your body, be aware of your breathing, and see the environment.

You may not be able to get it at the first try, but you can always try again. Remember, practice makes perfect!

Chapter 11: PEACE AND TRANQUILITY

Peace is a state of harmony and amity where things are calm, less complex and stress free. Peace could be the manifestation of quietness or stillness both of man and his environment. It could also be the inner state of mind of a human person that extends to external consciousness of how that man reacts and relates to and with his immediate environment. It could be expressed in a human being by the realization of inner joy or bliss through the acceptance and surrender to the environment and situation where the person finds himself. This therefore means that Peace as a concept operates both in the physical connotation (i.e., the environment and situation that a person finds himself at a given point in time) and abstract connotation (i.e., the inner joy and bliss experience by man through the acceptance of the environment and situations that he finds himself at every point in time). This means that peace could be internal or external. It is internal where it exists within a human person, and external where it relates to the immediate environment of the human person.

Tranquility is a serene state that is untroubled and less perturbed. Also, tranquility, just as peace, could relate to an expression of calmness or stillness. It could also relate to a state of human mind which deals with equanimity. To this end, we can safely refer to tranquility as a state of peace of mind of a human person when it is independent of external conditions and circumstances and exists within. The terms, peace and tranquility are therefore interwoven and could be used to describe and explain each other.

Peace and tranquility in relation to the subject matter of this paper can be narrowed down to peace of mind, which is the common term that is used to explain the state of being mentally or spiritually at peace, with enough knowledge and understanding to keep oneself strong in the face of discordor stress.It has also been explained to mean being healthy due to the absence of mental stress and anxiety (peace of mind is considered to be the ideal remedy to stress and anxiety). When the mind is calm and quiet, fears, worries and stress are prevented and this helps a human person to be confident and attain inner strength or find resolve in himself.

Chapter 12: The Use of Mindfulness

Mindfulness — self-perception and self-empowerment

Your mind shapes the way you perceive absolutely everything — what happens to you, what occurs around you. Most importantly, your mind controls your own perceptions about yourself. This directly affects your sense of self, and in turn how you experience yourself in the world.

Through societal norms and the media, we have been conditioned to believe that we need to look, act and live in a certain way in order to be successful human beings. At the same time, this means that we are all striving towards a man-made 'ideal' or 'perception', rather than following our own truth and embracing our own individual needs, gifts and beauty.

This societal 'brainwashing' has gone so far that we judge ourselves, and rather harshly, when we do not live up to the standards advertised all around us. We continuously compare ourselves to the 'ideals' laid out before us, leading to self-criticism and negative feelings about who we are and where we are in life. It is in this place of self-judgment that we develop insecurities and a 'perception of lack', because we are not living up to what we believe to be the standard.

But when you take a step back, out of your mind and away from that conditioning, and just focus on yourself for a second, you'll begin to realize that you are a unique individual. There is no one in the world, now or in the past or in the future, who is exactly like you. Isn't that something? There is only one you, and there will only ever be one you. You have something to offer to the world that no one else can ever offer. That's truly incredible and just shows how immensely special you are.

When you shift your perception away from the societal conditioning, choosing to move away from the 'ideals' and 'standards' imposed upon your life, you'll shift from a perception of lack to a perception of uniqueness. Through awareness, you can change your entire experience of yourself, from self-judgment and inadequacy to awe, love, magnificence, gratitude and acceptance. And when you perceive – or rather believe – yourself to be a unique, one of a kind, magical being, your confidence and belief in who you are will naturally increase.

How does this all happen? How do you make the shift? How do you move away from the negative advertising of the self into a space where you are able to accept and love yourself as an individual? By using the power of mindfulness, of course. By practicing mindfulness, you'll hone the skill and power to shift your perception in every moment. You'll have the ability to change a negative perception of yourself into a positive, loving and empowering perception.

When you are empowered in your individuality, and not comparing yourself to others or standards or ideals created by the media and society, you can fully share your authenticity with the world. A gift that no one else, except you, can bring to the table.

Likewise, we need to be aware of the same in others. We cannot disempower ourselves and others by being in a judgmental space. When we judge others, we take away their right to be themselves and we dampen their ability to give of themselves authentically to the world. Remember, judgement comes from preconceived notions of how we believe things should be. And mindfulness teaches us that we can change those notions at any given moment, simply by choosing to do so.

In each moment, you have a choice. You can choose how you react or act in any given situation, and this is where your power lies. You can get angry, frustrated or even despondent when something goes wrong. Or you can see the situation for what it is, accept it and then move on into your preferred state of being. That is the power you possess. You can choose, at any time, all the time, how you want to be — irrespective of external forces.

Mindfulness and the liberation from limiting belief systems and patterns

As we learnt earlier, everything we do, think and feel in life is shaped by our belief systems and thought patterns. Why do we work? So that we can make money to buy things and sustain our lives. Why do we wear clothes? Because walking around naked is not socially acceptable. Why do we choose the clothes that we wear each day? Because the fashion trends say so. The type of food we eat? It's what we've always eaten. The length of our hair? It's how it's always been. The fact that we brush our teeth, get married, have children, drive a car... We live our lives doing all these things, not stopping to question why we are doing them in the first place.

As we are conditioned to do all these things, we are also conditioned not to question what we do and why we do it. This doesn't have to be the case. Mindfulness teaches us that we can make conscious, informed decisions about absolutely everything in our lives. We don't simply have to continue doing what we're doing because it's the way it has always been done. We are not following a predetermined path where tomorrow already exists – tomorrow is created by the thoughts, actions and decisions we make today.

At any given moment you can walk, talk, sit, stand, run, jump, clap, laugh, cry or even move to another country – just by choosing to do so. Now you can see how much freedom you have once you accept that the choice lies with you, not society, not your parents, not your friends, not others – but you and you alone. How you live each moment is entirely up to you.

Your reality is up to you. It is being created through you and the current state of being that you choose to be in. If you never consider changing anything, you never will. If you never consider that you want to do something else with your life, you never will. And all it takes for you to make the bold decision to live the life you choose is a moment of consideration. A moment where you acknowledge that there is a bigger cause, a bigger meaning to the life you have been living — a life more aligned with your true chosen self.

Start by being aware of your thoughts. Then become conscious of the decisions you make in every single moment. Change your thoughts, change your actions, change your reactions, change your perceptions, and soon you will be walking a completely different path of your own choosing.

Here's an example. Let's say you want to change a belief system from 'I am unhealthy' to 'I am healthy'. First you need to become aware that you carry around the non-serving belief that you are unhealthy. By identifying the harmful belief system, you are in a position to choose what you would like to do with it. In this case, you want to change it to 'I am healthy'. In order for this to now become an experienced reality, however, you need to take on the new belief as your truth. This will immediately bring about positive emotions, and your new belief system will then prompt new actions, such as eating healthily and perhaps doing some exercise. When first changing belief systems, daily affirmations of the new belief, 'I am healthy', can help the process of conditioning the mind to align with the new chosen belief.

Mindfulness and self-responsibility

Mindfulness is the acknowledgement that we're responsible for everything that we experience in our lives. We are 'poor' only because we perceive ourselves to be so; we are 'ugly' or 'stupid' because we perceive ourselves to be so. From another's perspective, we may be wealthy, beautiful and intelligent. An unsuccessful relationship or unhappy marriage can be the result of certain beliefs about ourselves, our partner or our life that create frustration or dissatisfaction in the relationship. Similarly, we're unhappy or happy in our jobs because of what we believe about the job, ourselves and our life. Once we realize that our beliefs create our experience of our reality, we can take responsibility for ourselves and our lives.

The truth is that it is 'easier' not to take responsibility for ourselves and our lives. It's simpler to continue being a victim, blaming everyone and everything else around us for our misery and misfortune. We then continue with our lives, coasting along with a certain level of dissatisfaction, day after day, for the rest of our lives. But when we become mindful that our reality is created by everything that we say, think and do, we quickly realize that in each moment we have the power to create the reality and life experience we prefer.

Easier said than done, right? But practice is all that we need, and any moment is as good a moment to practice these tools.

Take a short moment to pay attention to your breathing and let go of distracting thoughts by acknowledging them and focusing back on your breathing pattern. Now realize the power that this very moment brings. This very moment is unique and new – it has never happened before and it will never happen again. And soon it will be replaced with a brand-new moment, totally unique in its own way.

Take a moment after reading these words to close your eyes. Focus on your breath. With each breath that you take, consciously choose to come back to focusing on your breathing, as thoughts will engage with you in order to get your attention. Simply acknowledge these thoughts and tell them to come back later. Focus on your breath again and do this until you reach three full breaths uninterrupted by your thoughts. Your focused attention is one of the greatest forces out there.

Remember, where attention goes, energy flows.

Let us take the example of a husband coming home from work to his wife and children. He's had a long day at work, the traffic on the way home way was crazy and he's tired and hungry.

Scenario one: The husband parks his car, marches inside all flustered and asks his wife if dinner is ready. She explains that she has not yet started cooking; the husband gets upset and they start fighting. The children hear their parents arguing and they get upset, and so the atmosphere becomes increasingly negative on account of the husband's state of being.

Scenario two: The husband parks his car and acknowledges his current state of frustration, owing to the challenging day he's just experienced. He chooses to take responsibility for his current chosen state of being and stops to take a few deep breaths. He chooses to change his perception to one of gratitude, giving thanks for his job, his car, his family, his house. He realizes how blessed he is. In this state of gratitude, he walks into the house and goes up to his wife to hug and kiss her, and they share stories about the day. The children hear that their father is home and they come to say hello, and the whole family catches up and decides what they would like to have for dinner.

The outcomes of these two scenarios show us how we are responsible for our own state of being. We also see how our words, thoughts and actions affect the people around us. In each moment we have the choice to be happy or to be angry, to take our frustrations out on the people around us or to realize that our frustrations are created by ourselves because we believe things should be a certain way. When we believe things should be a certain way and we have expectations of the future or other people, we will always be disappointed and frustrated. Expectation, after all, is the master of disappointment.

We see once more that it is our chosen perception that creates our experience. It is our responsibility and our gift to the world to become aware of the ways in which our thoughts, words and actions shape our life experience and affect and shape the life experiences of those around us.

Chapter 13: Beginning Your Mindfulness Adventure

Mindfulness isn't some kind of a course where you can practice for a few months and then live with bliss for life – it's the adventure of a lifetime, an everyday thing, part of your living. If you're a sailor, mindfulness is your boat, without which you just cannot discover unknown gems in life. Imagine that you want to sail, you have a boat, but you're not sure what you're going to find or where you're going in the first place. But isn't that what excites people more; the fact that the whole trip is a surprise?

When you start your mindfulness adventure, you will experience a lot of surprises, things you never knew you could do, and you will also experience anxiety – the time when you'll worry about how long the good feeling will last. It's only natural. Let me give you an example here. When I started my mindfulness journey I thought I had the whole world in my hands. I finally felt I could deal with things better, and this feeling gave birth to anticipation and I started becoming curious. Because we're humans, and as I've mentioned before, we make mistakes, there were times I felt unsure about being mindful.

I was never encouraged; nobody cared to tell me if I had improved, so I began questioning my focus, discipline, and will power. Somewhere at the back of my mind I knew I was doing it right, but my feelings were powerful enough to shadow the victories I had achieved. This is normal, and also another reason why I wrote this book – to help you overcome those feelings. The problem I faced was simple – I knew mindfulness was the only way for me to heal physically, mentally, and spiritually, but I was too concerned about the goals I wanted to meet.

Every time I wanted to achieve mindfulness, I thought about its impact on my goal – what was going to happen, how I was going to react, and if the consequences might be different. While mindfulness does help you achieve your goals, focusing too much on your goals isn't advised. To be mindful is to be alert. How can you be alert if you're focused elsewhere? Remember, mindfulness is process-oriented, not goal-oriented. You can only do one thing perfectly at a time, if you multi-task, you might finish all the things, but the quality wouldn't be as you would normally expect.

If Mindfulness Is A Boat, Your Mind Is A Sea!

When you start something new, you're always going to be excited at first, but as time goes by your excitement will wear off and you might come to think that maybe mindfulness isn't helping you at all. You might wish to go back to your life and live the way you normally would without mindfulness. What first started out as an exciting journey soon became gloomy and boring – this is normal too, so if you're suffering from this, my advice is to just hang on to mindfulness. I was starting to sense a resistance whenever I decided to sit down and meditate, sometimes the reasons were silly like, maybe I should walk the dog first and then meditate; or even sillier, let my downloads finish, and then I'll start.

Instead of giving in to the resistance, try overcoming it, and when you do, you will feel awesome! It's a feeling you have never imagined, it's like defeating your weak-self to give way to a stronger one!Also you must stop limiting your mind and restricting yourself. If you start your meditation process with sentences like, "I should do this and I must do it right," "I'm going to focus 100%," or "I'm going to try very hard to do this," you're already limiting your mind to do the right thing.

Not only are you restricting yourself, but indirectly you're pressurizing yourself and setting high expectations – something you can't achieve in the beginning. What happens when you do this? In the beginning, after restricting myself like that, I felt that even after minutes of meditation I wasn't feeling any better, in fact I felt worse. Why? It's simple. The entire time I was meditating, I was focused on focusing! Because I was focused on the wrong thing, not only did it let me down, but my mind went crazy.

Wait, when I say crazy, I don't mean I lost my marbles (!) I'm sane, but what I was trying to say is that my mind was all over the place. Thoughts from yesterday came back, today's pressures, tomorrow's deadlines all came to haunt me mercilessly. That's when I realized that it wasn't the mat, or the floor that was the problem, the problem was with what I was focused on. As soon as I corrected that, my mind became calm, I started seeing through things, I started making better decisions because in the end, nothing got me by surprise. Nothing made me cringe. I wasn't as stressed out as I was before starting the adventure and, well...people did see the difference.

On Your Mark, Get Set, Focus!

When you sit to meditate, don't restrict yourself. Instead, accept the thoughts and focus on one at a time. Try and bring an act of kindness and curiosity, and acknowledge your experience.

Remember, you can't be perfect so don't try too hard and never give up; you will achieve mindfulness if you stop trying and just go with the flow. Your mind has a mind of its own, so it will wander. Let it wander – it's part of the process, let it free. When it comes back, it will be rejuvenated! Once you understand and embrace these golden nuggets, you'll see how easy it is to meditate and achieve mindfulness without limiting or restricting yourself. Don't cling to anything – watch, observe, and let it go. It's the only way to peace!

Exploring Mindfulness with a Somewhat Thought-Free Mind

When you get the hang of it, when you start seeing some benefits, you'll know that nothing else truly matters. It's like you've been sailing for so long and finally you see something beautiful, something that's familiar to you, but so different from how you thought it would be. You mind will literally be free from everyday clutter! You'll feel like a whole new person with a brand-new mind.

When you began your journey, your mind was full of thoughts, but when you return, it'll be clean, beautiful, calm, and peaceful – and it's your home – from where you first began. The journey doesn't end here; this is just the beginning, because this journey is never-ending. It's full of possibilities, full of new emotions, new experiences, and new challenges.

After achieving mindfulness, you'll learn how to be alert, to be attentive and never to live in the past. You'll be a living example of a "happy go lucky" person who is fun to be around. Although there will be times when you feel that you might have lost your grip, you'll still know how to get it back without much effort. The everyday ups and downs, the pains and pleasures will not bother you much because every day, for you, will be a happy day.

Chapter 14: Uniqueness of Living in the Present

Living in the present is definitely easier said than done. After all, everyone has a past,

and sometimes, that past could really mess up with the present. But here's the thing: by

allowing the past to mess with the present, you kind of get to ruin the future a bit because

you keep living in the past. You don't offer yourself a chance to be redeemed and forgiven for your past transgressions - even by yourself.

If you don't forgive yourself for the past mistakes, then you will develop the feeling that

the whole world has conspired against you. You may have done your best, but nothing good happens. Such are the days when you have the feeling that there are no chances of succeeding again.

Well, guess what? You can definitely move past this awful moment in your life and become the kind of person that you have always wanted to become - or maybe even someone better than that.

What needs to be done?

Keep in mind that you have to assess the situation. You have to ask yourself questions

such as:

What can I do to make it better?

What makes me feel bad about this situation?

What went wrong?

When you determine and understand where things went wrong, and the gravity of a

situation, it becomes easier to know and understand what you need to do for things to be right. You can't escape or ignore your problems. Instead, you have to face them head on to avoid things becoming worse.

Start planning about what you can do to rise up from the fall. Others write about their

plans, make lists, or even make use of corkboards where they can pin write-ups and

photos of their plans. If you can visualize something, it has more promise of coming true. This is because if the mind can see something, it becomes more inclined to achieve it.

For instance, you lost some of your savings/funds and after that you plan this excursion

you should go on. You, additionally, have more plans to make money and saving the

more. When you understand that you have every one of these plans, you'll be more

energetic about working or doing whatever you can to save. To some extent, it makes things simpler rather than simply floundering in your circumstance and doing nothing about it. Along these lines, you can make things right and you are also ready to enable

yourself to improve and be a better and stronger person.

Chapter 15: The Mindfulness Shortcut– Travel

Have you ever thought you needed a change of scenery in order to feel better? It worked wonders for me, and I think it might work for you too. If you're feeling stuck and that the environment you are in is not supporting your needs, sometimes it is best to remove yourself from the place and find somewhere that works better.

Some people think of traveling as escapism, but actually, the opposite is true. When you travel, you are forced to be in the present moment at all times. You are faced with new, different, and exciting plans and opportunities that could change or shift at any moment. You break your daily routine in search of something new. Something different, exciting, or unplanned could happen at any moment!

When you travel, you are in charge of the decisions you make. If your bus or airplane is late, you have the choice to get upset or simply take this as an opportunity to rest or do something else in the meantime. When you travel, you consciously put yourself in situations that may, at times, be uncomfortable. Maybe you are traveling alone for the first time ever and have to get used to eating dinner alone. What feelings may arise during such a situation? If you think less of yourself because you are alone, are you able to work past that feeling? You can find respect for yourself for taking that chance and accepting your independence and ability to eat alone. You can acknowledge that there is, in fact, nothing wrong with eating dinner by yourself.

Mindfulness, however, begins at home, before your trip. You must ask yourself: Where do I want to go? What do I want to pack? How do I want to travel? If you feel stuck on making a decision about something- meditate on it, take a few deep breaths, and see how you feel about one or the other. Learn to trust your gut and go with your instincts.

> "The journey of a thousand miles begins with a single step."
> — Lao Tzu

When planning your travel, you may want to choose a destination or country that can support your mindfulness habits. Perhaps you choose to visit temples in Thailand rather than the hedonistic Full Moon Party. You may want to splurge on a resort or private room, or maybe you choose a yoga retreat. When your budget calls for it, you may even spend the night in a hostel. Making these choices in the moment, as you go, can sometimes be uncomfortable or put you in uncomfortable situations.

But you do not have to go to a so-called 'spiritual' destination in order to travel mindfully. Maybe it is something thoughtful, like going to visit your grandmother over in the next city. It doesn't have to be a far-away place.

What does this have to do with anything?

Traveling is like a never-ending ephemeral moment in time. When things don't go as planned (late bus causes you to miss your flight), you have a choice to respond by throwing a fit or calmly rescheduling your flight. Which sounds like the better option? No one wants to stress their nervous system even more from an already stressful ordeal... right?

The Effects of Stress on Your Body

Stress releases the hormone cortisol, which activates your body's 'fight or flight' response. This is a part of the sympathetic nervous system, which is a primitive system that evolved to protect early humans while developing hunting skills to remain alert from attacking animals and other dangerous situations. It was designed to protect the body from perceived threats. Here's what happens when the SNS kicks on:

Accelerated heart rate

Pupil dilation

Increased sweating

Constricted blood vessels

Elevated blood pressure

Decreased digestive function

Increased adrenaline

That doesn't sound like too much fun! These are not good for your body and can lead to symptoms of stress such as:

Headaches

Insomnia

Depression

Anxiety

Shallow breathing

Lowered immunity

Acid reflux/heartburn

High blood sugar

High blood pressure

Stomachache

Erectile dysfunction

Missed menstrual cycles

Lowered libido

Tight muscles

Mood swings and irritability

For these reasons, it is important to manage your stress in a mindful way... before things get out of control. Travel is good because it both gives you opportunities to get out of your routine and relax, and throws you plenty of curveballs that you will learn to handle once you get used to them.

Chapter 16: Mindfulness for All

Through the cultivation of mindfulness, a greater awareness emerges and so students switch into attention mode deliberately and at will, enjoying the present moment, experiencing compassion and curiosity. Even those who tend to worry about the future or remain fixated on the past will find that mindfulness can help. It's about tuning into thoughts, emotions and actions and by practicing the ability to stay in the present, there is less temptation for distractions.

While some people find it difficult to remain in the present, here is a useful mindfulness exercise to start with.
Task:

Ask students to close their eyes and to focus just on their breathing. Talk through how they need to focus on the inhalation, how the breath feels– whether warm or cool and to listen to the sounds that their breathing makes. They should be aware of how the chest expands and contracts. Then focus on the exhalation and how this feels. Students should try to focus on this for one minute.

This may sound easy but it is worth discussing the technique with students afterwards to see whether anyone struggled to stay fully tuned into this experience. Many of the students will slip into a distracted mode and this is quite common. If you find that students have struggled, repeat the exercise again.

13 year old students will have an approximate attention span of 39-65 minutes and 16 year olds, 48-60 minutes.

During this time, they are likely to be distracted if momentarily, but mindfulness helps them to increase their ability to focus, to learn and to stay in the moment.

Students are constantly distracted on a daily basis. They use social media daily and so read emails, messages, updates and phone calls constantly. With an increased or over-flowing schedule, distractions can chip away at their ability to stay in the present and to concentrate. By introducing mindfulness in a positive manner, it's possible for students to embrace and enjoy the richness that everyday life can present.

Research has indicated that mindfulness is often associated with higher emotional intelligence and so the individual has a greater awareness of their thoughts, feelings and actions. Importantly, they also understand the impact of how they think, feel and act in relation to those around them. Research has also indicated that by daily practice of mindfulness over a period of time, there has been a natural decline in the prevalence of stress and of emotional disturbance. From a school perspective, there is also evidence that mindfulness actually helps to increase the density of the brain in relation to memory, will regulate emotions and, learning. There are also physical benefits too, greater positivity and improved immune function meaning that students stay healthier for longer periods of time.

The benefits of being aware

As students participate in the mindfulness tasks, they will become more aware of what is going on in both the mind and the body. They don't just participate in any experiences, they truly live it and feel it. As such, there is less tendency for them to respond to situations on autopilot and instead of exaggerating potential problems by allowing negative thoughts to fuel reactions, they are instead able to create some space between a problematic experience and the reaction which leads to wiser responses.

Task

Hand out a sheet of paper to all students and asked them to write down a time where their inability to stop and think before reacting has caused a problem. This may be an experience which occurred at home or at school. Clarify that discussions will be discussed afterwards so they should only write something down which they are willing to share with others. This is a useful task which enable students to appreciate the link between negative thoughts and behaviours with emotional responses.

In these early learning stages, it is possible simply through discussion to help students identify negative behaviours already learned through childhood experiences up to the present date and to be able to take steps to change them if necessary.

We all learn from authority figures - parents, teachers, our peers etc. Lessons learned are not always 100% accurate and group discussions and the analysis of how we think, feel and act often shine a light on everyday behaviours that could become problematic in time to come.

Because awareness is interlinked on an integral level with the practice of mindfulness, by opening up the potential to communicate with each other and to embrace the clarity of thought, students are being mindful.

When students are fully involved in a specific task-be it creative, practical or academic, they are being mindful. Often students will have a tendency to link mindfulness only with meditation and this is not the case at all.

Mindfulness isabout paying attention and it's about having the ability to avoid distractions from external or internal triggers. Here are some tasks that proves the distractions of the mind:
Task:

Read a short extract from a novel (aim for five to ten minutes approximately) and students should be listening carefully throughout. At the end of this reading session, students have to write down everything that they can remember about the story. They can do this in bullet format so it is easy for you to go round the class and to see how much information has been gleaned from those listening to you.

Note: it is a good idea to not clarify that this is a mindfulness task beforehand as when students feel they are being tested, they are likely to listen more intensely. It can be beneficial to test this out by reading an extract of the same story for another five minutes and to then see how much more has been absorbed. You can then explain to your class that they were much more mindful in the second session.

Task:

Mind chatter is often a problem and so ask students to empty their minds and to sit still for one minute. They are to think about nothing at all but to just develop an awareness of how they are feeling. The awareness should be on the breath and the body and thoughts should be carefully pushed back if they try to intrude. Afterwards, ask students to discuss how often thoughts popped into their minds during this one minute period. Explain that this serves to increase their awareness of how thoughts can detract from their ability to stay mindful even for a short period of time.

Regular practice of mindfulness enables individuals to slow down brain chatter and to halt any automatic responses which may be emotional and negative rather than positive reactions, aiding feelings of well-being and balance in life.

Thoughts will always creep unbidden into the mind, but it's how we respond to these thoughts that count.

Mindful creativity task:

Set up an art session and hand out paper and all equipment for drawing and painting. Explain to your students that is not about creating a work of art as such but rather about their being uninhibited with the use of colour, lines and creativity. The experience must be mindful and with attentive awareness. Think of it as doodling but with intent.

The sessions can be open in terms of theme or you can choose topics and just see what emerges from this uninhibited creativity.

Note: Ensure that the students remain engaged within this project. Mindfulness is for all. There is no religious components and the benefits are mainstream.

Chapter 17: Why Being Mindful Is Beneficial

Those who practice mindfulness have reported, amongst others, some of these benefits: self-control, improved self-discipline, higher tolerance, objectivity, higher emotional intelligence, and an improved ability to relate with self and others with more kindness, compassion, and acceptance.

Let us look at some of the scientifically proven benefits of being mindful in detail:

Reduces Anxiety

According to a study conducted by researchers at Massachusetts General Hospital, about 93 individuals suffering from diagnosed generalized anxiety disorder were randomly assigned to an 8-week control group, stress management education (SME) or group intervention with Mindfulness-based stress reduction (MBSR).

At the end of the 8 weeks, the group assigned to the mindfulness-based stress reduction showed significant reduction in their level of anxiety as compared to the group assigned to the SME group. Anxiety is a major cause of stress, and a significant reduction in anxiety marked a reduction in stress levels.

Helps you deal with stress

According to a study conducted by Professor Adam Lueke at Central Michigan University in 2015, engaging in mindful meditation can help you deal with stress caused by biases in the workplace such as race bias.

In this study, a group of white participants engaged in mindful meditation while a second group listened to a behavioral control audio. Professor Adam Lueke then asked the participants to look at a group of pictures of people from different races and choose which ones they favored to win a lottery. The participants who listened to the control audio all favored the whites in the pictures while the group who engaged in mindful meditation favored both the whites and the colored people in the pictures to win the lottery.

This shows that when people engage in mindful meditation, they tend to be more accepting and less judgmental of others, which will help encourage love and reduce bias-induced work-related stress in the workplace.

Treats Depression

Those who engage in mindfulness-based cognitive therapy (MBCT) combine both mindfulness-based stress reduction (MBSR) and cognitive behavioral therapy (CBT) to fight depression.

According to professor Willem Kuyken from the University of Oxford in the United Kingdom, engaging in MBCT helps people fighting depression recognize what is happening around and within them, which gives them the ability to respond and engage the triggers differently.

MBCTis an 8-week group-based program that exposes you to mindful exercises such as yoga, daily mindful homework such as bathing, eating, cleaning, washing, and several other household chores that help you pay attention to whatever you are doing, moment-by-moment; keeping depression at bay helps you fight stress more effectively.

Increases Your Level of Acceptance and Satisfaction about Your Body

Body dissatisfaction is a major cause of stress in women. Ellen R. Albertson, Kristin D. Neff, and Karen E. Dill-Shackleford, conducted a research study in which a group of women battling stress from body dissatisfaction and low self-esteem engaged in a meditation intervention group and another group acted as the control group. The group assigned to a meditation intervention group showed more self-compassion, self-worth, and body appreciation than the group acting as the control group. This clearly shows that practicing mindfulness meditation makes you more accepting.

Before we discuss the various mindfulness techniques, you can practice at home, work, on the road, and anywhere, let us look at how mindfulness helps relieve stress:

Chapter 18: Practicing Mindfulness Meditation

I have devoted a longer section to this because it's complex when you first start. Meditation takes place in a place where you won't be disturbed. You need to be comfortable and the clothing you wear should never be restrictive. Often people make a space devoted to meditation because this needs to become a daily thing. In fact, the more often you do it, the better you get at it.

Meditation is teaching the mind to react in a certain way, but instead of allowing conscious thoughts to come and go as they please, you direct them by letting go. Of course, in the initial stages of meditation, you are going to find that you do have thoughts wander into your mind. It's bound to happen so don't think you have failed just because this happens. I will teach you how to let go of those thoughts as we go through the meditation process.

Assuming you don't do yoga and don't know complex poses such as the lotus position, it's better to start your meditation by sitting in a hard chair with your feet flat on the floor. Your back should always be straight for a very good reason. This allows energy to flow through your body. Your strongest hand (i.e. your right hand if you are right handed) should be placed on your lap palm upward with your other hand placed on top of it – similarly palm upward and your thumbs touching.

Breathe in through your nose to the count of seven. Hold the breath to the count of four and then breathe out to the count of eight. Do this several times until it becomes a natural rhythm. Your inward breaths should always be through your nostrils.

Now, continue to do this, with your eyes closed. When other thoughts come into your mind, simply acknowledge them and don't address them with emotions or give them any real credence. Don't judge the thoughts. Imagine them drifting away like a piece of paper floating away into the air and go back to concentrating on your breathing.

You may wonder what meditation does but it is helping you to discipline your mind so that you can let go. You don't have to hold onto thoughts, and if you do this every day, you will even find yourself doing this when thoughts enter your head during the day that really add nothing to the moment you are living in. I do it all the time and am very conscious of doing it. Don't keep harboring thoughts in your mind because when you do that, you give the mind very little time or energy to enjoy what is actually happening in your life in this very moment in time.

It also helps you to sort your life out. Meditation is a kind of switching off, while being very mindful of the processes that happen in your brain. If you keep letting thoughts invade and don't discipline them, you end up with all kinds of negativity that comes from being overwhelmed when you really don't need to be.

After Meditation

You need to let your body get back to its normal state slowly. Write down what you can do better the next time you meditate to make your next session even more fruitful. This gives your heartbeat and your blood pressure a little while to get back to normal.

Meditation will help you to be more aware of what YOU are doing to make your life so sad. When sad thoughts come and go through your mind, let them go. They are only there while you allow them to be. If it isn't adding to your joy in that particular moment, get used to letting go. It is only by harboring these thoughts that anxiety and stress happen.

Chapter 19: Using Mindfulness to Become Happier, Peaceful, and Focused

In addition to curing conditions related to depression, anxiety, and stress, mindfulness can also infuse happiness and peace in your life. It can cure your physical conditions and enhance your emotional, mental, and physical well-being by manifolds. Here is how:

How Mindfulness helps you Become Happier, Peaceful, and Focused

In terms of affecting happiness, focus, and peace in your life, mindfulness has the following positive effects.

Mindfulness Alters Gene Activity

Dr. Bruce Lipton, a renowned developmental biologist, best recognized for publicizing the notion that your beliefs can manipulate your DNA and genes, states that the gene activity occurring in your body changes daily.

If your perception reflects on your body's chemistry and your nervous system can read and interpret everything in the environment, as well as control your blood's chemistry and structure, it is logical to conclude that you can actually alter the destiny of cells in your body by changing your thoughts.

Dr. Lipton's work clearly illustrates that if you positively alter your perception, you will be capable of changing how your genes behave. This control effectively enables you to bring changes to the numerous variations your genes bring into your body on a daily basis. This in turn means that if you can change your thinking pattern, you can make your genes behave how you want them to, and prevent them from bringing disastrous changes such as tumors and cancer in your body.

Moreover, you can use your thoughts to effect the 'nocebo effect' that often takes place in your body when you are diagnosed with a deadly disease, or receive news of your impending death. The nocebo effect causes you to pay heed to negative thoughts that make you believe in your impending death.

By learning how to control your thoughts, you can easily neutralize the nocebo effect, thus increasing your lifespan, as well as gaining complete peace of mind. Dr. Lipton also states that the best way to gain mastery of your thoughts is through mindfulness. Therefore, if you want to enjoy a full life, try mindfulness.

Mindfulness Techniques for Happiness and Complete Well-being

We have discussed Mindfulness based meditation in a previous chapter. If you continue with that, you can slowly gain control over your thoughts and use them to your advantage.

We shall not go back to that. Instead, in this bit, we shall discuss a few more mindfulness techniques (so you have a variety of exercises to try, and choose from). The idea is to infuse mindfulness in every aspect of your life, so that whatever you do and wherever you are doing it, you are fully alert, conscious, and aware of every tiny thing happening inside and outside you. The more mindful you are, the easier it will be to disconnect from negative thinking and worrying, and enjoy the present.

Mindful Immersion

Mindful immersion helps you to become fully engrossed in the present moment. It helps cultivate full contentment in your present, so you can escape the constant striving you routinely become caught up in.

If you observe yourself while performing routine chores, you will realize that you anxiously want to complete one daily chore so that you can move on to another. This makes you impatient. You are always in a hurry and are never able to get deeply involved in one chore at a time and enjoy its completion.

You start working like a robot whose sole job is to get things done on time. This routine makes things annoying and tiring for you. To escape this monotony and exhaustion, practice mindfulness immersion to help you find relief from the habit of worrying about things 24/7.

How to Practice Mindfulness Immersion

To practice mindfulness immersion, get started on a routine chore. For instance, if you start cleaning your room, do it in detail, and pay complete attention to every minute detail of this task.

Do not treat it as a routine chore. Rather, change it into a new experience by observing every little aspect of the actions you perform as you perform the task. If you are sweeping the floor, become involved in the sweeping motion and feel the movement of the broom as you move it. Sense the muscles that become involved in this act.

The more engrossed you become in this simple chore, the more relaxed you will feel. You will find the pressure of working like a robot slowly sliding off your mind and body. Moreover, you will become creative with the practice and maybe come up with an exciting new way of sweeping the floor.

Similarly, try this technique with every routine chore you engage it, be it reading a book, cooking, or making your bed. This simple practice, if adopted for good, can help you become calm, serene, and happy and when this happens, you can easily control your thoughts and influence them.

Mindful Appreciation

Mindfulness appreciation is a simple, but truly effective practice that helps you become more cognizant and appreciative of the gifts you have in your life. By recognizing your blessings, you become thankful of things you have and start becoming peaceful with loses. When the grief associated with losing things and people starts diminishing, your mind, and thoughts start grounding in the present. Here's how you can practice mindful appreciation.

How to Practice Mindfulness Appreciation

To practice mindfulness appreciation, start by noticing any five things that normally go unnoticed and unappreciated; these five things can be people or objects. Make a daily practice of noticing five new things and jot them down in your journal. When the day ends, understand the importance of these five things in your life, appreciate them, and express your gratitude for them.

These things support your existence and are important to a healthy living, but since you are always striving for bigger, better, and more luxurious things and lifestyle, you fail to recognize these important things.

Your list of things could include; electricity, water, air, house, pots, and pans, your postal worker, your plumber, your organs, your body, your five senses, your parents, your siblings, and several other important things and people similar to these.

After identifying the five things, dig deeper into them and find out how they came into being, what benefits they provide you, and how difficult your life can become without those things. This will help you truly understand their significance and be thankful for them. Make sure to practice this exercise daily, so that you can appreciate your life more and start living it fully.

Mindful Awareness

Mindful awareness is an exercise that cultivates heightened appreciation and awareness of the simple chores you perform daily, and the results you achieve with them. The aim of this practice, like all the other mindfulness-based exercises, is to ground you in the present so that you can control your thoughts and make them live in the now and not the past or future.

Here's how you can integrate this exercise into your life.

How to Practice Mindfulness Awareness

Think of an activity that takes place several times a day. The activity could be as simple as opening a door, holding your laptop, or drinking water. Next, when you engage in that specific activity, become more mindful of it.

For instance, if you are opening the door, become mindful and alert of where you're standing, the doorknob you are touching and how you are feeling. Appreciate the fact that this door leads to somewhere and gives you an exit point.

Apply this technique to your thinking pattern. Every time a negative thought enters your mind, pause for a moment, think of a suitable label for it, such as unhelpful or unhealthy, and then release it. Whenever a positive thought enters your mind, label it too, and then appreciate it. By doing this, you will be appreciating, and becoming aware of what you have, and will be releasing negativity from your mind as soon it enters it.

Practice these three mindfulness exercises to enhance your well-being and achieve a state of blissful happiness.

Chapter 20: MINDFULNESS MEDITATION BENEFITS

Many people have this notion that mindfulness meditation is difficult and can be performed only by those who have gifts of extreme concentration, focus and determination. Ironically, it is not that those who have these qualities only can meditate but actually people who meditate attain all these qualities in due course. Mindfulness meditation not only brings these three qualities in us, it also endows us with numerous other benefits. Let us discuss these in detail.

Individual benefits

relief from stress

A great scholar said,

"When I think back on all the things that have gone wrong in my life, each was the result of not paying close enough attention."

Stress is processed in our brains almost exactly as it was processed since the beginning of time. When your boss yells at you, the amygdala fires crazily and makes you feel the "fight, flight, or freeze" process in the same severity that we experienced when our main source of stress was finding caves to hide in, while lions and tigers were attacking us. We have socially evolved light years beyond our mental evolution. Honestly, we're still back in the stone age when it comes to processing stress.

Most of us feel that relaxation means sitting like a couch potato in front of the television at the end of a tiresome day at work. Ironically, this is the worst way to combat stress. In order to get over stress, we need to activate our body's natural relaxing responses which can be done by practicing mindfulness meditation. Meditation and deep relaxation techniques like breathing exercises can bring you back to level and even bubbly and more active. It not only boosts your physical energy, but also your mental energy.

After learning the art of mindfulness meditation, it is common for practitioners to feel less stressed and to notice that they deal more calmly with tense situations. When stress is reduced in the nervous system during mindfulness meditation, benefits like better sleep and clearer thinking also develop naturally. Many research studies have verified that the daily practice of mindfulness meditation produces a wide range of positive effects on a person's mind, body, and behavior.

Furthermore, this kind of mindfulness meditation is a great chance to spend some leisure time with ourselves in solitude. This allows us to be introspective and look within. Spending 15 to 20 minutes in a calm and breezy atmosphere with a relaxed mind practicing mindfulness meditation can do wonders and change us to efficient decision makers at work.

improves brain functioning and intelligence

Mindfulness meditation makes our mind sharp. Mindfulness meditation practices increases our IQ levels in various ways. It enhances our emotional intelligence by giving us the skills required to handle chaotic and stressful situations. It helps us in developing inner intelligence. It also synchronizes the left brain and the right brain and allows them to work more efficiently. Also, consistent practice of mindfulness meditation creates a thirst for gaining knowledge and improving current situations in life.

Mindfulness meditation even helps you develop intuition and consequently increases the internal intelligence. While this type of intelligence can't be judged with question and answer sessions, it is without a doubt valuable at all walks of life. This stimulates insight, creativity, and understanding and helps you to see beyond just material facts. Regular mindfulness meditation will give you the skills to listen to your feelings, then work through them in a calm, thoughtful manner. Many who have lived their lives ruled by anger learn through mindfulness meditation how to put anger aside and handle situations rationally.

As a whole, it is a definite truth that mindfulness meditation can make you more intelligent from the inside out.

improves creativity

Creativity comes in our childhood. This is what is most popularly talked about as right brain development for kids of different age group. The right brain functions are not stimulated by normal functions and activities kids follow in school and at home. It needs special efforts in way of specific games, creative arts and well-thought out sets of activities to improve and stimulate creativity. Mindfulness meditation is one such activity to improve right brain functioning.

It was a strong belief from ancient times that creative geniuses are born and not made. People believed that creative qualities were innate in geniuses. But mindfulness meditation has proved that creative geniuses can be made.

Mindfulness meditation creates the mental and emotional conditions in which creativity is most likely to flourish.

better focus and concentration

Concentration can be defined as having unwavering focus. Concentration becomes hopeless when we get distracted by several different things at the same time. In order to improve our concentration, we must stop trying to do several things at a time. If this one-pointedness is developed, we will gain a new energy to complete any kind of task in hand with better pace and accuracy.

The main obstacle or block to one-pointed concentration is unavoidable distractions that we face through our numerous thoughts. This obstacle can be overcome only when thoughts are silenced and controlled. And what better way one can find apart from mindfulness meditation to control thoughts.

improves interpersonal skills and helps build good relationships

Just a few minutes spent daily taking care of oneself by practicing mindfulness meditation increases one's capacity to respond to the needs of his or her friends, family and colleagues. It is saidthat 'The best way to help others is to first help oneself'.

"You reap what you sow." This is considered to be the fundamental principle in everyone's life. It is very true that people respond in the same manner as we respond to them. Relationships are like mirror reflections. If we are more open and positive towards a person, he or she reciprocates in the same way towards us and vice versa. Mindfulness meditation helps develop this positive attitude in relationships and hence earns rewarding results in case of family business and other social relationships.

There is no doubt that one can easily differentiate a regular practitioner of mindfulness meditation from a normal person. They always approach everything differently from others with a cool head. Also, the maturity in their behavior and strong personality makes them stand out, and they gain an automatic respect and attraction from people around them.

Reduces anger

We rarely realize the effect of our anger on the victim. If you wound a person physically, it can be healed with medicine; but a heart wounded by anger is harder to heal.

The great Dalai Lama has said,

Chapter 21: Practice Mindful Observation and Listening

Quite often, the things we see and those that we hear are influenced by our experiences. The preconceived notions that we have built over time influence our perception of almost everything. If you have had a bad episode with a donkey, you may find every donkey annoying. If you don't like a certain person, you will never listen to him/her with an open mind and will always be skeptical of what he/she says even if he/she is saying the wisest thing ever.

Naturally, when you see and hear things with a skeptical mind, it is very difficult for you to be mindful of them and when you aren't mindful of your surroundings and your feelings, you are quite likely to fall in the stress and anxiety trap. To keep this from happening, train yourself to observe and listen to things mindfully. Here is how you can achieve this goal.

How to Practice Mindful Observation

· Pick a natural object from within your surrounding environment and then place all your concentration on it for a few minutes. You could pick a leaf, a flower, an insect, clouds, the sky or anything else you feel like observing.

· Set your timer for 2 to 5 minutes or even 10 if you can observe something peacefully for that long.

· Breathe mindfully for 2 minutes before you start observing that object. This calms you down and prepares your mind to be more mindful of your surrounding environment.

· Now start observing that object and look at it very gently. Simply relax into observing that object for as long as your attention allows.

· Observe it as if you are seeing it for the very first time and take interest in it.

· Visually explore the different aspects of its formation and structure. If you are observing the clouds, see how they move around or how fluffy they seem. Try to look at them from different angles and you are bound to find something new and special about them.

· Think of how that natural object affects the world and let go of any preconceived notions and judgments that you have formed about it previously. Just focus on how amazing it is in its own special way and you will find yourself becoming more involved in it.

When you finish observing the object, write down your findings in a journal and go through that account. If you find any sort of judgments, observe the object again and try to observe it more non-judgmentally. Think about why you feel judgmental of it and what made you think of that critical viewpoint. You will soon realize that you thought that way mainly because of a preconceived notion. Breathe deeply and try to eliminate that preconceived notion and accept that object openly.

Carry out this exercise every day and after 2 weeks of doing it, do it twice or thrice a day. Within a month, you will start looking at everything with a more open and accepting eye and will start becoming more mindful of everything.

How to Practice Mindful Listening

· Select a song or an instrumental piece of music that you have not heard before to listen to it with an open and clear mind. Try not to choose a song by an artist you don't like or someone you like to ensure you have a more clear and unbiased viewpoint of the song.

· Put on the headphones and close your eyes while listening to the song.

· Try not to be drawn into judging the song in any way based on its title, the artist's name or the genre of the music before the song has begun. If you find yourself putting any sort of labels on the song based on its title, gently bring your attention to your breath. As you breathe deeply and mindfully, you will start to let go of the judgments you formed as well and will become more nonjudgmental of the song.

- As the song plays, let yourself become involved in it and explore every tune, beat and lyric. If you seem to dislike any aspect of the track, let go of your initial dislike and keep exploring it. Allow your awareness to move into the song and dance to the sound waves.

- Separate the different sounds you hear in your mind and assess each one of them individually.

- The more you explore the track non-judgmentally, the more you will start to enjoy and appreciate it.

Once the track ends, write down your views or your journal and go through them a few times. Assess any judgment you formed based on your preconceived notions and let go of them just as you did when observing a natural object mindfully. The idea of this practice is to listen very intently and to become completely entwined with the composition of the song without any preconception of anything related to it.

Practice this exercise a few times and then start listening to the people around you mindfully as well. You will be surprised at how unbiased and open you will become in a matter of days. If earlier you used to feel angry listening to a certain person, now you won't feel that way anymore because now you will listen to him/ her openly and non-judgmentally. Practice mindful listening as much as you can and soon you will listen to every sound and word with an unbiased and clear mind.

Now that you have become better at listening and observing things, practice mindful awareness and immersion to become more aware of the things around you and start to do things with increased awareness too. The next chapter will focus o these practices.

Chapter 22: In Your Mind's Eye

Aside from reciting positive affirmations, another great way to practice mindfulness in winning the war against stress, anxiety and depression is visualization.Simply put, this is the practice of seeing yourself or your desired outcome in your minds eye with as much vivid details as possible.The principle behind this is that our minds tend to think better with pictures.And by visualizing those that are very important to you and seriously want to happen or achieve, you're able to program your subconscious mind to look for ways to achieve your visions.

You may not be aware of it but when you daydream, you're already practicing the mindful art of visualizing as you see in your minds eye those that you want to happen.But with visualization, more focus and attention on the things you want to "see" is needed.And how's it done?It's pretty simple:

Commit to setting aside everyday to practice visualization, i.e., seeing in your mind's eye what is it you want to achieve, particularly win the war against stress, anxiety and depression.Every day, one or two sessions of 5 minutes each should be more than enough to start with.

Find a quiet place where you won't be disturbed.Ensure the sacredness of that place.If it's a room, make sure to put a "Don't disturb" sign outside and lock the door.

Paint a picture or shoot a movie of those things you want to manifest in real life, e.g., being confident, relaxed, rested, and successful.With as much detail as you possibly can, imagine how it looks like when you've already one the battle against stress, anxiety and depression.

That's it – it's that simple!It's so simple that there's really no excuse not to do this exercise.

Chapter 23: Dealing with Distractions while Meditating

Despite having concerted efforts to maintain a state of mindfulness, the mind may wander. It may suddenly jump to past or anticipated experiences--a novel you read long ago, friends not seen for years, a future meeting, a trip on the coming weekend, etc. The moment you notice that your mind is no longer focused on your breath or body, consciously bring your mind back to meditation. Below are some suggestions to aid you maintain the concentration needed for the practice of mindfulness.

1. Counting

When you are distracted, counting may help. Its purpose is simply to refocus the mind on your breathing. Once your mind is refocused, give up counting. There are numerous ways to do this and they should all be done mentally. Some of the techniques are as follows:

a) While inhaling, count "one, one, one..." until fresh air fills your lungs. While exhaling, count "two, two, two..." until the fresh air empties your lungs. Then while inhaling again, count "three, three, three..." and "four, four, four..." upon exhalation. Count until ten and repeat until the mind is focused on the breath.

b) The second technique is counting quickly up to ten. Breathe in while counting "one, two, three, four,... nine and ten" and again breathe out while counting "one, two, three, four,...nine and ten". Do this again as many times as necessary to focus the mind on the breath.

2. Connecting

Do not wait for the brief pause after exhaling but connect the exhaling and inhaling. This lets you notice both breaths as one continuous breath.

3. Fixing

After connecting your inhalation and exhalation, fix your focus on the point where you feel that your inhaling breath and exhaling breath touch one another.

Notice your breaths moving in and out, rubbing, or touching the rims of your nostrils.

4. Focus the mind like a carpenter

When a carpenter wants to cut a board, he draws a line on it. Then by using his handsaw he cuts through the board along the drawn line. His focus is not on the teeth or the saw as they shift in and out of the board. Instead, his entire focus is placed on the line he has drawn so he could straightly cut the board. In a similar fashion, you should keep your focus straight on the spot where you experience your breath coming in contact with the rims of your nostrils.

5. Your mind acting as a gatekeeper

A gatekeeper would not notice the specific details of people. His attention may only be focused on the general movement or number of people going in and out of the house through the gate. Likewise, during mindfulness meditation, do not take into consideration any specific element of your experiences. You simply focus on the feeling of your inhalation and exhalation as they enter and leave the rims of your nostrils.

With continuous practice, you will have a light feeling in your mind and body. It feels so light that it seems you are springing towards the sky or floating on water. After your gross in-breaths and out-breaths abate, subtler breathing follows. When a sign-object appears for the first time, a subtler sign-object will replace it. You can compare this subtlety with the ringing of a bell.

When someone strikes the bell with a huge iron rod, there is a gross sound heard at first. Eventually, the sound fades and becomes extremely soft. Just as with your practice, the first few in-and-out breathings appear as a gross sign. With more and more attention placed to breathing, the sign becomes so subtle. Meanwhile your consciousness stays completely paying attention on the rims of your nostrils.

As the sign develops, more objects of meditation become clearer and the breath becomes subtler. It will become so subtle that you will not anymore notice the existence of your breaths. At this point, do not be disappointed thinking nothing is happening to your practice because you lost your breath. Do not worry and just be determined and mindful enough to bring back the sensation of breathing at rims of your nostrils. This is the time you must perform more vigorous practice, balancing your mindfulness, self-trust, patience, determination and wisdom.

Chapter 24: Practicing Mindfulness

Mindfulness is a journey whose destination is Here and Now

Mindfulness is the mental frame defined by awareness and acceptance. The contents of this text are for the attainment of this perspective. Just as we can train our muscles with exercise, we also have the ability to train our state of mind. Where we once allowed our minds to be passively pulled by past matters, we will now actively direct them towards a more centered focus.

Imagine that Mindfulness is a tower rising to the stars, a structure we are building from moment to moment. Every time we make the decision to act mindfully, we lay another brick to strengthen this tower's foundation. At first our tower may be small and fragile, falling to the blow of the gentlest winds. But as it is is rebuilt and fortified by our Mindful choices, it will come to prevail against the strongest of gales.

The more that you are Mindful, the easier it becomes to stay Mindful and the harder it is for your peace and personal power to be swept away. Therefore the goal of entering this state day by day is not to simply serve as a routine against emerging negativity. Attaining Mindfulness is about bringing more awareness into your everyday, average experience of the world.

Not long after you start your practice, you will notice some distinct changes in your awareness. You will become calmer, less driven by harmful emotions, and find that everyday matters which used to be stressful can no longer knock you off-balance. This is the purpose of Mindfulness practices: training a balanced state of mind. By entering this state during your Mindful sessions, you will have access to Mindful thinking in everyday situations.

Though the realms of mind and emotion are often regarded to be immaterial, the power of the following practices are more than wishful thinking. There has been extensive scientific research into

Mindfulness practices which have identified its positive effects on stress.

What stands behind our stress response is not a single area in the brain, but a network of brain structures connected as a system. Mindfulness alters how this network interacts, directly changing our experience of stress. The foremost of these structure is called the Amygdala which is strongly connected to emotional processing. Mindfulness leads to lower activation in the Amygdala in response to a wide range of stimuli. Lower activation means less emotional reactivity and the emergence of a balanced mental state.

By reducing the activity in the Amygdala and increasing activity in the logical centers of our pre-frontal cortex, Mindfulness practices rewire our brains the moment we begin to undertake them. Training the attention to our bodies, thoughts and emotions increases the brain density in those areas in which we focus. This means that we expand our awareness as we are aware, bolster our memory as we remember and improve our conscious control as we control it. Mindfulness ultimately causes a new paradigm to arise in the mind. A hierarchy in which we are rightfully on top, guiding our thoughts and feelings instead of being guided by them.

Imagine a stressful encounter on any given day. You know that you are irritated on your conscious level. There are some roots of your irritation you are unaware of -- such as gloomy weather -- on your subconscious level. While Mindfulness introduces a third level above them both that can be described as Meta-Consciousness. This level is the awareness of your state of awareness. It is the perspective of a witness observing everything that is occurring at a conscious level and evaluating what is happening at the subconscious level.

From this level of objectivity you will wield immense personal power.

This power will be a reflection of your peace of mind.

This peace is cultivated though Mindful practice.

The Breath Awareness Technique

Using your awareness to direct your thoughts and emotions can be quite the endeavor. Luckily this path that has been walked by some of the greatest minds throughout human history. Controlling the breath is a time-tested techniques for increasing the ability to focus our attention. There is a Sanskrit term called Pranayama that means "control over the breath". The techniques of Pranayama, which can be found in ancient meditation manuals, capture the essential link between our rate of breath and our state of mind. The moment we slow down the breath, the pace of our thoughts slows down as well.

The uses of Breath Awareness extend well beyond the mind; we can influence bodily systems that aren't voluntary control. A fine example is the regulation of the pulse. The mechanism of natural arrhythmia occurs with every breath: when we exhale, our heart rate gets slower than when we inhale. By making your exhalations slower, your pulse will slow down as a direct result. This is a fundamental relaxation technique with great utility, one that you can practice at any moment.

1) Sit it in comfortable position on the floor or a yoga mat. Place a cushion or a folded blanket under your pelvis, it will make sitting straight much easier. Adjust the height of the cushion to your needs. The key here is comfort.

2) Place your palms above your knees, straighten your spine, lift up the sternum, and roll your shoulders back, moving your shoulder blades closer together. Make your neck straight, take a single deep breath and exhale slowly...relax. The key to getting a proper posture is relaxing the muscles while keeping a straight spine. Think about the muscles in your back and your shoulders. Are they tense? Try to let go of all the tension.

3) Close your eyes and focus on your breath. You don't need to breath deeper. Accept your breath as it is and simply observe. Begin by bringing your focus to the tip of your nose. Observe your breath at the tip of the nose. What kind of sensations do you have? Can you feel the gentle movement of the air coming in and out of your nostrils? Practice that for a few minutes.

4) Now observe your breath passing through your nose. Feel the air brushing against the back of your nostrils. Notice, that the air you exhale is warmer than the air you inhale.

5) After a few minutes, shift your concentration to your throat and observe your breath passing through it. Gently tighten the muscles of your throat to feel the movement even more. You should be able to hear a delicate, hissing sound.

6) Now take your awareness to your chest. Observe the breath as it enters and exits. Feel it expanding and contracting. Experience the movement of your ribs.

Notice that your shoulders are slightly rising with every inhalation, and relaxing as you breathe out.

7) Finally, concentrate on your abdomen. Feel the movement of your diaphragm as it draws the lungs down inflating them and then squeezes the air out. Notice the movement of your abdomen as it expands with every inhalation. Feel your navel drawing towards the spine every time you exhale.

Enjoy the calming effect this breathing exercise has on your mind. The more of your awareness that you focus on breathing, the less intrusions will arise in your mind. Focusing on your breath may feel a bit unnatural at first but will be honed through practice into a vital tool of Mindfulness.

The Observer Technique

This exercise is designed to help us develop greater awareness of the body. It also serves as preparation for Mindfulness Meditation. By training daily you will gradually acquire a passive awareness of the state of your body and its needs. Creating this attunement and listening to your body will allow you to recognize the situations when it is stressed and identify the areas where you are tense. You will be able to release this tension with little effort or consciously correct a posture that puts strain on your spine and your muscles. All in all, step by step, you will learn how to improve the way you carry your body around.

Naturally, your posture and bodily state is closely linked to your state of mind. Whenever we are stressed we have the tendency to tense up. We assume a defensive position, subconsciously lifting our shoulders to protect the head and close ourselves to the external offender. When we are happy and relaxed our posture opens up. The muscles relax, the spine lengthens and we stretch to occupy more of the surrounding space.

Like the breath, this mechanism works in both ways. Just as the state of mind affects the posture, you can influence your state of mind by Mindfully changing the position of your body. The next time you are stressed, pay attention to how your body responds. Take a few deep breaths. Release the tension from your shoulders. Lift your sternum slightly up, make your spine straight, and relax your abdomen. You will feel an immediate and potent difference.

1) Set an alarm for ten minutes and lie down on your back. The Observer Exercise is performed best this way so that you won't need to worry about passing time. The mattress of your bed may be a bit too comfortable and make you more likely to fall asleep. Using a yoga mat on the floor is recommended.

2) Spread your limbs as wide apart as you can, your arms out to the sides of your body with your palms facing up. Stay completely motionless without changing this initial position.

3) To conduct the Observer Exercise you must silently monitoring your flowing stream of consciousness. You will find that thoughts will continue to come and go

without any effort on your part. Simply observe the thoughts as they pass by.

4) Acknowledge the thoughts about the bodily sensations you are experiencing. Can you describe the feeling of your back pressing against the floor? What about the weight of the Earth's downward pull? How do your clothes feel against your skin? Observing the words that we use to describe these physical sensations reveals the link between how we think and our perception of what is happening.

5) Remain still and acknowledge distractions instead of reacting to them. Some parts of your body may start itching or aching after some time. Arising with these sensations is the thought of discomfort, prompting you to change your position. . This inaction will bring you to a mindful realization. You will understand that your actions are not tethered to every thought impulse in your mind. Observing and allowing these feelings to pass without acting on them illustrates the crucial power of choice that you wield in every moment.

The goal of the Observer Exercise is to demonstrate this power to you and cultivate an understanding of its use. You will then be able to apply it when confronted with matters that you feel trigger the burdens of Stress, Anxiety, and Fear. Watching your thoughts without reacting to them shows you that you can remain unattached. The influence a thought has on your actions is the influence you allow it to. Realize that the decision to provide the physical effort and energy behind every arising thought is yours and yours alone. Those that you act on are those that grow stronger.

The Observer Exercise leads to greater Mind Awareness. You will begin to recognize its movements, habits and rhythms. As you excel and become better at the Observer exercise, you will come to better understand and appreciate the complexity of the ways we use thought to interact with the world. You will find that your very focus on your thoughts and sensations it what intensifies them and gives them a stake in reality. With this heightened awareness of the mind's inner workings comes a heightened level of control.

The Body Scan Technique

While the Observer Exercise concerns matters of the mind, the Body Scan is a tool for recognizing and directing the processes in your body. It is unique in how it utilizes the power of visualization. The Body Scan will put you into a state of deep relaxation. Your mental faculties will slow, but you will remain conscious. If you happen to become so relaxed that you are falling asleep you can complete the exercise with your eyes open.

1) Set the alarm clock for 20 minutes and assume the same position as the Observer Exercise: supine, arms and legs spread apart, palms facing up. Remember, that you should remain motionless throughout this exercise. Release all the tension from your body. Think about your back, neck and your shoulders – any part where you accumulate and carry stress. You will

gradually scan your body part after part by shifting the concentration of your focus

2) Bring your awareness to your right foot and think about how this area feels. Do your toes feel warm or cold? Can you feel them touching each other? Anchor your mind in this location and imagine a feeling of warmth and relaxation starting here. Think about this sensation getting warmer and slowly spreading through the entirety of your foot.

3) Imagine this warmth and relaxation spreading further up your leg. Relax your ankle and shin and feel the sensation travel up an inch at a time to your knee and thigh, feel your vessels dilate as your blood moves to nurture every part of it. You will feel that your whole leg is warm and relaxed. Acknowledge how heavy and motionless it is.

4) Now take your awareness to the toes of your left foot. Again, try to deeply feel this area. How do your toes feel? Can you feel them touching each other? Anchor your mind in this place. Imagine a feeling of

warmth and relaxation starting here. Imagine your toes getting warmer as the feeling slowly spreads around your foot. Visualize this until your foot is completely relaxed and you can imagine it radiating with pleasant warmth.

5) Imagine this feeling of spreading further up your leg to pass through your ankles and shins. Notice your calves become completely motionless, pressing against the surface you are lying on. Visualize this relaxation traveling inch by inch to calm your knees and your thighs. Your blood vessels dilate to increase circulation in your leg until you feel they are both warm and relaxed. Notice how heavy they feel without moving.

6) Now take your awareness to your left palm. Feel the back of it touching the surface you are lying on. Anchor your awareness here and start the visualization. Imagine a feeling of warmth and relaxation radiating from the center of your palm and slowly filling all of your fingers. Feel your entire palm become warm and relaxed.

7) Envision this feeling spreading through your arm toward your shoulders. Relax your wrist and feel the warmth moving as it passes through forearm and elbow to voyage further upward. Soon, you can feel that your whole arm is warm and relaxed. Feel how heavy and motionless it is.

8) Take your awareness to your right palm. Anchor your awareness and examine the feelings arising here. Imagine a feeling of warmth and relaxation radiating from the center of your palm and slowly filling all your fingers. Feel that your entire hand is warm and relaxed.

9) Watch its spread through your arm as it moves toward your shoulders. Relax your wrist and feel the warmth passing through your forearm and elbow to voyage further upward. Feel this warmth and relaxation radiating from all of your limbs. Acknowledge their heaviness, as if sinking into the floor. Notice how completely motionless they are.

10) Concentrate on the center of your chest – the area of the heart and sternum.

Feel your heart pumping, acknowledge its rhythmic motion, and sense it coursing blood through your body with every beat. Imagine a feeling of warmth and relaxation radiating from your chest and spreading around your torso. Slowly relax your entire abdomen from the top of your neck to the bottom of your groin.

11) Have the feeling travel to your back, feeling it become more warm and relaxed. Imagine yourself sinking into the surface you are lying on.

12) Direct this wave of relaxation up the back of your neck, feel it entering and filling your head. Relax your chin and your mouth, your nose and your cheeks, your eyes up to the top of your skull.

13) Finally feel the relaxation of your entire body while remaining motionless in this visualization. Pay attention to your slow, deep breaths. Imagine that with every exhalation you become more relaxed, that with every breath you sink deeper and deeper...

When mastered, the Body Scan is an excellent relaxation practice. Beyond its Mindful value, it can serve in place of a nap. Relaxing your body with the Body Scan technique will leave you as rejuvenated and full of energy as any brief period of rest.

Chapter 25: How to Make Meditation a Habit

Now that you've had a crash course on the benefits, history, and various techniques of meditation you are ready to go forth and make meditation a daily habit, sounds easy right? Unfortunately creating lasting habits is an art of its own and requires its own set of skills. You will need to put in the effort upfront to build them, but that's okay because you already know everything you have to do and all the things you want to try in your meditation practice now you just need to know how to make meditation a habit with these helpful ideas.

Know Why You are Deciding to Start a Meditation Practice

With any new habit knowing your "why" is crucial. You need to have a strong response when your resistance to the new habit pops up, and it will initially so arm yourself with a personal reason for why you are getting into this. Some excellent reasons would be "I'm not getting quality sleep and it's stressing me out so I'm meditating before bed to calm my mind and help me fall asleep." or "I'm feeling unproductive at work and am meditating to improve my focus so I can work toward that raise I want" other reasons which might not have the same lasting effect would be "I saw it on Instagram, so I want to do it too" or "My partner is pushing me to try it, so I might as well" You can see the different motivating factors in these statements, make sure that your why is strong enough to push you past your resistance.

Create the Habit

Creating new habits is hard, it's not impossible but you have to have a strategy to get you from where you are now to where you see yourself with your "why" statement above. There are entire books written on this subject and countless studies on the science of human behavior but thankfully these studies can distill the subject down to a 3-step cycle.

The 3 R's of Habit Change

To successfully implement a new habit all you need is 3 steps:

1. Reminder – the trigger that initiates to behavior

2. Routine – the behavior you perform

3. Reward – the benefit or reinforcement of that behavior

For your practice instead of relying on motivation, which can be fleeting instead tie your reminder to something you already do automatically and let that be your trigger to meditate. Say you brush your teeth every night you can use that as your reminder - brush teeth, meditate, sleep. This way you can insert your practice into an existing habit.

For the routine set your goal small, this seems counterintuitive to the "Dream Big" and "10X" mentality of some personal development teachings but it is better to do a small amount of meditation consistently every day than to sit for an hour one day and then drop the habit.

Write your goal down where you see it every day if your trigger is to meditate after brushing your teeth put your goal on a sticky note above your toothbrush. It has been scientifically proven that the odds of you achieving a written goal is astronomically greater than the odds of you doing something you've just kept in your head. Write down what you're going to do (i.e.: mindfulness meditation for 2 minutes) on that sticky note and stare at it while you brush your teeth - or whatever you decide on for your reminder.

By setting your intention for 1 - 3 minutes to being with you know you have no excuse to avoid just 2 minutes of meditation and as you develop you can always add more but start here until the practice becomes an automated part of your day.

When you are forming a new habit, you have to make it a priority and schedule in a specific time to do the new thing. This is where tying it to an existing habit is helpful because until you've done it enough times to become automatic you will forget to do something that only takes 2 minutes, and you may need to rely on your trigger for a long time, that's perfectly ok, do whatever it takes to make meditation a part of your day. If you prefer to fly by the seat of your pants and are not into strict schedules you still need to set a soft deadline for your new habit. The good thing about starting your meditation practice is you can stop in your tracks and take 2 minutes to meditate. The important thing is to make doing it a non-negotiable, it doesn't matter if you missed your trigger or if you waited until the very last minute, as long as you can say you did it and enjoy one of the rewards your allocated to yourself then you will be doing the work to form a new habit.

Saving the best for last, the reward at the end of your behavior is what will turn this experiment into a lifelong habit. You will feel the benefits of meditating, even for just 2 minutes but to cement a new habit into your psyche you need something extra to encourage you back again and again. Create a reward that celebrates your achievement - and yes, meditating for 2 minutes is a huge achievement, be proud of your commitment!

One method is simply positive self-talk, at the end of your meditation say out loud "yeah you did it!" or "nice work, good job, you rock" whatever gets you pumped. You can put a checkmark on your calendar for every day you meditate, the human brain is somewhat simplistic and the act of checking off something you've done gives you a small dose of the feel-good chemical called dopamine, do this enough and your mind associates meditating with that dopamine hit and you are set. Depending on how you schedule your practice you could use an hour of watching your favorite show as a reward or enjoy a delicious cup of tea, which works great in the morning, maybe you want to put on your favorite song and have a dance party for yourself. Create a reward for yourself that you look forward to receiving and you will never have to rely on motivation again.

Follow these three steps for 3 to 4 weeks and you will find you have created a new habit. It takes approximately 21 days to form a new habit and with the positive benefits from daily meditation and the fun rewards you've given yourself you will be pleased with your results, but don't stop there! Track your progress from day 1 with a checkmark in your calendar for every day you meditate, once you've reached your 30-day goal you will have a chain of checkmarks to look back on and feel proud of and now moving forward your only job is to not break that chain. It is inspirational to look back on the effort you put in and allow that to act as a pre-reward for continuing with your practice, see how far you can make the chain last and set the intention to give yourself a bigger reward after 365 days of meditation.

Simple Mindfulness

So what if you've read this far and you still think you don't have time to meditate (trust me, you do, but that's ok) you can still incorporate the concepts into an incredibly informal practice of simply being mindful in everyday occurrences. You don't need a special room, or a timer or a mantra to meditate, remember? All you need to tap into the benefits of mindfulness is your attention.

Mindful Meditation Before a Meal

You have to eat, right? How about taking a few moments to sneak in some mindfulness to your day? Practicing a moment of mindfulness before a meal and paying attention as you eat can lower your stress levels and help calm the mind, it will also help improve your relationship to food and can improve your digestion. When you bring your attention to your food and how it's making you feel you provide the opportunity to truly connect to the process and pick up on the signals your body is giving you, like "I'm full" or "this food doesn't agree with me."

As you sit down to enjoy a meal pause for a moment and feel grateful for the food and the nutrients it contains. Say to yourself something like "I am grateful for the nourishment it is about to provide for my body." breathe deeply and intentionally take in the delicious smell, notice the beautiful color of the vegetables and feel gratitude for how well balanced it is. As you eat, take your time and fully taste each bite, be mindful of the textures and the different flavors. Make eating a meal a full sensory experience and as you eat slowly your body has time to react and communicate back to you.

You can take this idea back one step and as you are preparing your food, be present and mindful of how you are putting your meal together. Take time to create something you can look at with some level of joy. Choose the highest quality of ingredients that you can and selectively create a meal that you know you will feel good about.

Mindful Meditation While Walking

Anytime you find yourself walking somewhere for a few minutes you can practice a small meditation be being fully aware of all your surroundings, how your body is flowing through space and all the activities happening within your body at the present moment. As always, start by bringing your attention to your breath for a few moments. Then start from the ground up and shift your focus to your feet and how they feel on the ground, mentally scan up your body and see if you notice any tension or stiffness anywhere, take a few breaths to direct your energy there and try to release the tension if you can. Next, draw your attention to your surroundings. How's the temperature, is it cold, windy, muggy? What noises are happening all around you, see if you can differentiate what is happening beside you versus sounds come from behind you. What is catching your eye, is it a vibrant flower or a huge billboard, how do the colors make you feel, alarmed, soothed or nothing at all? Try to take in as much detail about your surroundings as you can, safely, of course, still pay attention to crossing the road or walking off a cliff!

Mindful Meditation While Inline

This method of mindfulness comes in handy when you have nothing better to do than wait. If you are stuck in one place, even for a few minutes you can sneak in some mindfulness. Avoid the urge to take out your phone and instead bring your attention to your breath and take in the sensory details of your surroundings. Check-in with your body, how is your posture? Are you putting all your weight onto one hip? Stand taller, drop your shoulders and tuck your pelvis in, not only will this make standing more comfortable it makes you appear taller and slimmer. Release the tension from your body and bring a smile to your face, even if you feel grumpy about having to wait, by being present and putting on a smile it will have an immediate effect on your mood. Notice if the people around you react differently to your energy, so they shift their bodies, does anyone else randomly smile? Observe your surroundings while you breathe slowly and you may just find some inner peace at the grocery store.

CHAPTER 26: UNDERSTANDING ANXIETY

Knowing what anxiety is, what causes anxiety, the symptoms, and the possible treatments is very vital if you want a healthy life. Though anxiety can be a normal aspect of our lives every time we receive a threat or face nerve-racking challenges like joining contests or speaking in front of your big bosses in the company, it can turn into a fatal condition where we seriously lose our healthiness physically and mentally. There will come a time that anxiety will no longer be a typical experience for you in particular situations, but a disturbance that interferes you anytime and anywhere.

What causes anxiety attacks?

Usual distressing circumstances like too many rush works to get done given a specific deadline to meet and managing family relationship conflicts is one of the main causes for developing anxiety. Getting caught up in these situations more frequent than you have expected can lead you to have anxiety that can already be hard to control. Many of us do understand that all these settings are typical part and parcel of life, but there are also many of us who are too frail and susceptible when it comes to experiencing these not easy sides of life. Thus, many have fallen to getting anxiety disorders. What causes anxiety disorders, therefore, are the ways how people treat and face challenges.

What are some of the anxiety attacks symptoms?

Some of the situations that will help you determine that you are experiencing anxiety attacks symptoms are when you feel your muscles vibrating and shaking, you're sweating too much and your start feeling hot in your face, ears, and neck, your fingers will start to numb and feel cold, you get to feel dizzy and feel like vomiting, you will experience a difficulty in breathing while your heart palpitates, you experience migraines, and start to feel strange and too emotional. More of these anxiety attacks symptoms include having a difficult time to sleep, you begin to have frequent bad dreams, you cannot control yourself anymore, and you feel suddenly fainting even when just relaxing. If you are experiencing all these possible symptoms even when you are not doing anything stressful and difficult, you may be are suffering from an anxiety disorder. The moment you think and feel that you have an anxiety disorder, you should immediately consult the right doctor; otherwise, your anxiety disorder will bring you to having a psychiatric problem. You should be able to distinguish possible anxiety attacks symptoms to right away provide some treatments that will perhaps get enable you to reduce the level of tolerance.

Controlling and Treating Anxiety

If you want to have a peaceful and healthy way of living life, then you should be very much willing and determined to stop yourself tolerating anxiety even if the procedure can be a little difficult to accomplish. One of the simple ways which everyone can do under anxiety treatments is to unwind and relax once a week or twice a month. If you just spend some time with families or friends in the park, in the mall or into relaxing places, you are helping yourself a lot in getting rid of anxiety. Stress is the main contributor to anxiety can be lessened if you try to go to spas or any relaxing venues where you don't have to think of your works and problems. Anxiety treatments can be effective is you will always thinking positive at everything you do. If you learn to accept difficulties in life and be always optimistic in doing things, you can get away with anxiety disorder. Try not to tolerate anxiety by staying calm especially when you have to finish a lot of works in a small amount of time. Anxiety treatments are the positive attitudes we need to develop particularly when dealing with difficult challenges in life.

The discomfort and fear associated with panic attacks gave them the right of a bad name. Few people know what causes panic attacks and this ignorance even live in constant fear of suffering from such attacks, in turn, makes them more vulnerable to severe anxiety. Before turning to see what triggers anxiety attacks, so we'll try to understand what an anxiety attack and what happens when a person suffers.

What is anxiety?

Anxiety often referred to as "panic attacks" in medical terminology are episodes of intense panic or fear, which occurs without any warning. On an average stretch of these episodes of panic a few seconds to about half an hour, with symptoms of anxiety peaked in the space of 10 minutes or more. The distress of the person exposed to the short period may prove to be a frightening and unpleasant. A person suffering from anxiety attacks are likely to feel as if he suffers a heart attack or a nervous breakdown. Some of the most common symptoms include anxiety attack increased heart rate, sweating, numbness, weakness in the knees, fear of dying, etc.

What causes anxiety?

It 's very difficult to determine the exact causes of anxiety attacks because they are often different from the person. The person likely to suffer from anxiety attacks when he does not know how to react to a given situation, as has been stuck in an elevator when the movement on stage, etc. In fact, fear is a major causative factor when it comes to anxiety attacks in children. Similarly, a person is more likely to panic when an important event such as losing a job or get divorced, change the course of life. Major events like the death of a family or large financial losses can also act as triggers such attacks. anxiety attacks are also common in people suffering from mental disorders such as obsessive-compulsive disorder and Post Traumatic Stress Disorder.

Other than the psychological reasons mentioned above and some physical factors also act as an anxiety attack triggers. Antidepressants and other prescription drugs that can disrupt the normal functioning of the brain can also trigger panic attacks in some people.

Sometimes, anxiety attacks episodes observed as a symptom of withdrawal from the addiction. This is not entirely surprising since people are so involved in their addiction that they just cannot imagine life without these drugs. There are also certain medical conditions, such as catecholaminergic polymorphic ventricular tachycardia (CPVT) and long QT syndrome, which can cause anxiety in individuals. Anxiety attack like during sleep due to conditions such as hyperthyroidism and vitamin B. While some sleep disorders like sleep apnea and Nocturnes vapor can trigger anxiety attacks at night.

In fact, anxiety is regarded as a symptom of this disease, and that a person experiences an anxiety attack must also be diagnosed with these disorders. Some people are more vulnerable to panic attacks from others and tend to panic about the events of very low life. It is very difficult to determine the causes of panic attacks in these individuals. Despite the panic attack is considered a hereditary problem, people with no family history of anxiety disorders may also suffer the same thing.

What to do during an anxiety attack?

As mentioned earlier, the anxiety attacks come on suddenly and so you have plenty of time to react. controlled breathing and distraction may facilitate the situation, allowing time to seek help by calling the emergency services. If you are prone to anxiety attacks, you can bring a paper bag with you. Breathe into this paper bag is one of the most effective methods of short-term treatment to relieve anxiety. On the other hand, if you're wondering how to stop the anxiety attacks at the same time, the answer is using a variety of psychological therapies and medications. In fact, cognitive-behavioral therapy (CBT) is considered the best treatment for various anxiety.

It was a brief information about what causes anxiety attacks, which belong to several factors that tend to provoke such an attack. Taking into account the seriousness of this problem, it is obvious that knows how to deal with anxiety attacks can be a blessing in itself.

Chapter 27: Mindfulness in the Workplace

There are times when colleagues really annoy you. Everyone feels like this though those who learn mindfulness are less prone to make it a priority and to thereby make their work life miserable. They know that they need to work to earn the money to live, but are able to see things in a better perspective. When given too much work, the mindful look at the whole situation without judgment or anger and try to come up with solutions. They know that anger serves little purpose and is one of the negatives in life that it's better to avoid. Thus, they may look at the amount of work that they have to do and prioritize rather than fill their heads with angry thoughts and achieve less. Yes, there is a lot of work, but with a positive outlook and a good head for prioritizing, they are able to achieve more. A typical conversation could be:

Boss: I need these done by five o'clock tonight.

Employee: I have a very heavy workload. Would you like me to give this work priority?

Boss: Yes please.

It's a very simple conversation to have and yet people get angry every day of their working life because they don't look for solutions to their problems, but highlight the problem itself. The solution is simple. Having asked the boss if this work takes priority over other jobs, his confirmation gives you direction. If the other work isn't done, then it's simply because of the order dictated by the boss and there's nothing to get angry or upset about. Be mindful as you work through that pile of items you have been given. Prioritize as suggested and enjoy your work without making worries in your head about whether you can get everything done. The positive attitude that you show in the workplace will give you superb results in that you are not letting anger, frustration or inadequacy get in the way of tackling the main job at hand. You will therefore work more quickly and will achieve more.

Getting angry in the workplace

This serves no purpose whatsoever. Let's take an average day in the workplace and show you how mindfulness makes it much more pleasant. You walk into the office – you greet all of your colleagues with a pleasant smile. You start your workload and sort it into priorities and you knuckle down. During the course of contact with others, always be aware that those people may have shortcomings but it's nothing to get angry about. Let them own their own shortcomings and learn to accept that not everyone is like you. Mindfulness means observation and you may find if you employ observation in the workplace, other people's shortcomings may be because of something you have done or not done. We had an office junior who came in every morning with a glum look on her face. She knew she was about to face another day of demands from everyone and that included me. She was the junior and we kind of treated her like one. When I observed how she was treated by everyone, including myself, there was hardly any wonder the girl was so unhappy. I adopted a new attitude toward her. I treated her as an equal and helped her to learn more so that she wouldn't always be in that junior position. The problem was that no one had ever trusted her enough to do anything but the mundane. As fate would have it, she was very talented at calculations and introducing her to a new job within the office – that took priority over getting everyone their coffee – she saved me so much time that I could make coffee occasionally for her. Although the boss was a little bit startled by this change in roles, he actually saw the benefit because our productivity doubled and none of us had to sit through this poor girl's unhappiness any more. When you are mindful of people and their needs, it makes you a better and more approachable person and can make the work situation a lot easier.

At one stage, I was given far too much to do. Instead of getting worried about it, I voiced my concern and people who had hardly ever spoken to me volunteered to help out, since their workload was less. An angry attitude would not have achieved the same result. Thus keep all negativity out of the workplace and make it a place where you are mindful of the following things:

- Your workload
- Your own capabilities
- Your colleagues
- Your boss
- The happiness factor

When you do, you will find that productivity rises and that people are generally much more approachable. Anger and frustration have no place in your life. Every moment that you spend in your workplace can feel like a life sentence, but it can for people around you as well, and most certainly will do for people who have to endure your angry thoughts. Thus, change your approach. Be happy and sharing in the workplace and you will find that people are naturally happy and sharing too. They don't want to spend their whole day in misery either and your mindfulness can help to end any negativity that you and colleagues have experienced and make the workplace a much more enjoyable place to be.

If you find yourself overloaded, ask for help. No one minds someone admitting that they have too much on their plate and often you can reciprocate when your workload is less and theirs looks a bit heavy. Mindfulness of each moment in the workplace makes you a friendlier person who people are not afraid to approach.

Chapter 28: The darker side of being mindful – and what to do about it

If I've given the impression that mindfulness and formal meditation are harmless and have no downsides, I'd like to clear that up here. When you meditate and when you teach your mind to become more alert to itself, you're taking a closer look at aspects of your inner landscape that may have previously been unfamiliar to you.

You may discover passions, questions, memories and parts of yourself you never even knew were there. Because being mindless can also serve a protective function, you may discover yourself exposed to some feelings you've actively pressed out of awareness. Asking the question, "who am I amidst this thought traffic?" can get you some strange answers. When you remove distractions and endless mental chattering, what's left?

For some people, beginning to meditate is the start of a bumpy ride. Leah, for example, may become aware that a big source of her unhappiness stems from an unfulfilling relationship with her partner. Her thought traffic protected her from this realization for years, so that when she finally let that traffic go quiet for a second, some very disturbing feelings emerged.

This is all normal. But be prepared for it. Be particularly careful if you suffer from anxiety or depression – although on the balance an appropriate mindfulness schedule will almost definitely have a benefit. When you get into the habit of experiencing the moment, as it is, rather than identifying with the empty words and symbols pointing to the moment, expect some intense emotions. Imagine Neo living outside of the Matrix – the present moment is cold, strange and a little harsh at first.

You may discover some old memories bubbling up during formal meditation. You may discover a dream you used to have but have since put to sleep. When you get deep down to work on your "self," expect that your opinions about things may change, and with them your goals. This is all grist for the mill. Whatever happens, maintain calm awareness and just be.

CBT and modern mindfulness

Many people have a knee-jerk reaction against mindfulness practice and meditation because they can't see the use of it – what are you actually doing? So what? You're just sitting, how does just sitting change anything?

I hope I've convinced you of the value of mindfulness so far – and if you've been practicing it yourself, you may know these benefits first hand. But it's true in a general sense that just sitting doesn't change the world or anything in it.

Though it's well beyond the scope of this book, this brief section will consider some smart methods people have developed to take the cultivated conscious mind and put it to good use. Mindfulness is brilliant for its own sake, but it also makes an excellent base from which to achieve other goals. As we've seen in the previous section, you may be wondering what to do with all the garbage you've found in your mind after you've become more aware of it!

Here I'd like to suggest (to those who are interested) a look at some basic cognitive behavioral therapy techniques, and how they fit seamlessly with the mindfulness techniques we've already considered.

The principle is simple. In cognitive behavioral therapy, thoughts (cognitions) affect behavior, so if we wish to change a behavior, we have to change the thoughts behind it. As we've seen, mindfulness practices are all about becoming aware of your thoughts.

If you're trying to break an addiction, overcome trauma, motivate yourself or resolve some personal issues, I strongly recommend you look for a CBT practitioner in your area, or else join a mindfulness based group. But because there's nothing like the present moment, here is an exercise you can do right now, in the spirit of blending mindfulness principles with those of CBT.

Step one: Become aware of your thoughts

Well, you should be getting good at this part! Literally write thoughts down, along with any accompanying emotion, if you like. For example, you might write, "I'll never succeed at anything at my age."

Step two: Look at the behaviors they cause

What happens because of this thought? Notice your response. Do you go out less, criticize yourself or turn down opportunities to try new things? Look at the emotion, too. You might feel sad, defeated or angry.

Step three: Decide to take charge

Are you happy with the result in step two? If not, commit to making a change.

Step four: Adjust your thoughts

"I'll never succeed at anything at my age" is probably not strictly true. Very few things in life are "never" or "always" true, anyway. Think of counter examples — there are many people who only achieve their life's work after 40 or 50. Is your statement an exaggeration? Is it even true? What is a more realistic alternative to this thought?

You might change this belief into, "I can always make good choices for myself, in the moment, no matter how old I am." This is not some fluffy positive thinking nonsense, but it will shift your emotions and hopefully, your behavior. You may be more inclined to try new things, push yourself, and recover from minor setbacks.

Step five: Reprogram yourself

If you are mindful, you can be aware when you start telling yourself, "I'll never succeed..." You can cut yourself short mindfully, and gently bring your focus to a new, more useful thought. Likely many, many times over.

Step six: Repeat

And keep going! Using a mindfulness based CBT technique like this takes patience and persistence. But it does work, and has been shown to offer substantial relief for people suffering from anxiety, depression, stress, eating disorders and more. Becoming mindful is a great first step to deliberately taking charge of your thoughts and by extension, the world around you.

Conclusion

Now you have all the basic information you need to start a beginner's practice. Remember that meditation can be as deep and encompassing as you want it to be. You can choose to swim on the surface of the lake, or you can choose to dive into the depths. It's all up to you.

Hopefully, this book has provided you with everything you need to nurture your practice and ease you into the wonders of meditation. As long as you can keep yourself motivated and focused on your practice, you are sure to see the physical, emotional and spiritual benefits.

www.ingramcontent.com/pod-product-compliance
Lightning Source LLC
Chambersburg PA
CBHW072004070526
44583CB00015B/1320